MW01233859

Key Concepts in American History

Progressivism

Set Contents

Key Concepts in American History

Abolitionism
Colonialism
Expansionism
Federalism
Industrialism
Internationalism
Isolationism
Nationalism
Progressivism
Terrorism

Key Concepts in American History

Progressivism

Reyna Eisenstark
with
Lora Friedenthal

Jennifer L. Weber, Ph.D.
General Editor
University of Kansas

Key Concepts in American History: Progressivism

Copyright © 2010 by DWJ BOOKS LLC

DEVELOPED, DESIGNED, AND PRODUCED BY DWJ BOOKS LLC

All rights reserved. No part of this book may be reproduced or utilized in any form or by any means, electronic or mechanical, including photocopying, recording, or by any information storage or retrieval systems, without permission in writing from the publisher. For information contact:

Chelsea House
An imprint of Infobase Publishing
132 West 31st Street
New York NY 10001

Library of Congress Cataloging-in-Publication Data

Eisenstark, Reyna.
Progressivism/Reyna Eisenstark, Lora Friedenthal; Jennifer L. Weber, general editor.
p. cm.—(Key concepts in American history)
Includes bibliographical references and index.
ISBN 978-1-60413-223-6 (hardcover)
1. United States—Politics and government—1865-1933—Encyclopedias, Juvenile. 2. Progressivism (United States politics)—History—19th century—Encyclopedias, Juvenile. 3. Progressivism (United States politics)—History—20th century—Encyclopedias, Juvenile. 4. United States—Social conditions—1865-1918—Encyclopedias, Juvenile. 5. Social movements—United States—History—Encyclopedias, Juvenile. 6. Social problems—United States—History—Encyclopedias, Juvenile. 7. Social change—United States—History—Encyclopedias, Juvenile. I. Friedenthal, Lora. II. Weber, Jennifer L., 1962- III. Title.
E661.E43 2009
324.2732′7—dc22
2009025284

Chelsea House books are available at special discounts when purchased in bulk quantities for businesses, associations, institutions, or sales promotions. Please call our Special Sales Department in New York at (212) 967-8800 or (800) 322-8755.

You can find Chelsea House on the World Wide Web at http://www.chelseahouse.com

Cover printed by Bang Printing, Brainerd, MN
Book printed and bound by Bang Printing, Brainerd, MN
Date printed: May 2010
Printed in the United States of America

10 9 8 7 6 5 4 3 2 1

This book is printed on acid-free paper.

Acknowledgments
pp. 1, 13, 17, 31, 41, 46, 54, 57, 67: The Granger Collection, New York; p. 20: AP Photo/ Mark A. Duncan.

Contents

Viewpoints About Progressivism

List of Illustrations

Photos

Maps

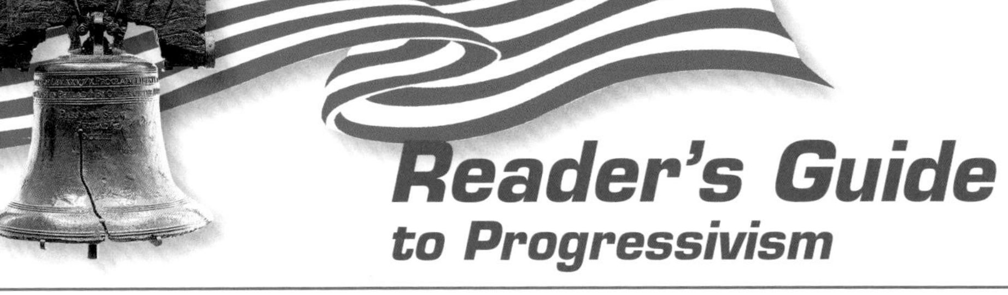

Reader's Guide to Progressivism

The list that follows is provided as an aid to readers in locating articles on the big topics or themes in America's Progressive Era of the late 1800s and early 1900s. The Reader's Guide arranges all of the A to Z entries in *Key Concepts in American History: Progressivism* according to these 6 **key concepts** of the social studies curriculum: **Conservation and the Environment, Economics and Trade Issues, Government and Law, People and Society, Policies and Programs,** and **Social Movements**. Some articles appear in more than one category, helping readers to more easily see the links between key topics.

Conservation and the Environment

Conservation
Muckrakers
Muir, John (*See* Theodore Roosevelt)
Roosevelt, Theodore (1858–1919)
Sinclair, Upton (1878–1968)
Taft, William Howard (1857–1930)

Economics and Trade Issues

Child Labor
Conservation
Food and Drug Act, Pure (1906)
Interstate Commerce Act
Payne-Aldrich Tariff Act (1909)
Roosevelt, Theodore (1858–1919)
Sherman Antitrust Act
Sinclair, Upton (1878–1968)
Taft, William Howard (1857–1930)
Veblen, Thorstein (1857–1929)

Government and Law

Anthony, Susan B. (1820–1906)
Bull Moose Party
Child Labor
Conservation
Eighteenth Amendment
Election of 1912
Interstate Commerce Act
Johnson, Hiram (1866–1945)
La Follette, Robert (1855–1925)
Marshall, Thomas (*See* Wilson, Woodrow)
McKinley, William (1843–1901)
Muckrakers
Nineteenth Amendment
Norris, George W. (1861–1944)
Payne-Aldrich Tariff Act (1909)
Progressive Party
Prohibition
Food and Drug Act, Pure (1906)
Rankin, Jeannette (*See* Suffragists)
Roosevelt, Theodore (1858–1919)
Seventeenth Amendment (1913)
Sherman Antitrust Act
Suffragists
Taft, William Howard (1857–1930)
Twenty-first Amendment (1933)
Wallace, Henry (*See* Progressive Party)
Wilson, Woodrow (1856–1924)
Woman Suffrage

People and Society

Addams, Jane (1860–1935)
Anthony, Susan B. (1820–1906)
Child Labor
Conservation
McClure's Magazine (1893–1929)
Muckrakers
Prohibition
Riis, Jacob (1849–1914)
Roosevelt, Theodore (1858–1919)
Sinclair, Upton (1878–1968)
Social Justice
Stanton, Elizabeth Cady (1815–1902)
Suffragists
Steffens, Lincoln (1866–1936)
Taft, William Howard (1857–1930)
Tarbell, Ida (1857–1944)
Temperance Movement
Veblen, Thorstein (1857–1929)
Wells-Barnett, Ida B. (1862–1931)
Wilson, Woodrow (1856–1924)
Woman Suffrage

Policies and Programs

Conservation
Child Labor
Food and Drug Act, Pure (1906)
Muckrakers
Prohibition
Suffragists
Temperance Movement
Woman Suffrage

Social Movements

Bull Moose Party
Conservation
Hull House
McClure's Magazine (1893–1929)
Progressive Party
Prohibition
Riis, Jacob (1849–1914)
Sinclair, Upton (1878–1968)
Social Darwinism
Social Justice
Suffragists
Temperance Movement
Woman Suffrage

Milestones in

The Progressive Era in the United States was a period of **reform** that lasted from the late 1800s to the early 1900s. Progressive reformers called for a wide range of economic, political and social reforms, or changes. During this era, investigative journalists called "muckrakers" exposed political corruption, unfair business practices, and social ills.

Initially successful at a local level, the reform movement spread to the states and the federal government. At the national level, reforms included the income tax (with the Sixteenth Amendment); direct election of senators (with the Seventeenth Amendment); Prohibition (with the Eighteenth Amendment); and women's suffrage (through the Nineteenth Amendment and the U.S. Constitution).

1869 Elizabeth Cady Stanton founds the National Woman Suffrage Association, seeking the right to vote for women.

1872 Suffragist Susan B. Anthony arrested for voting in the presidential election.

1887 Congress passes the Interstate Commerce Act to prevent unfair practices in the railroad industry.

1889 Jane Addams opens Hull House, a settlement house, in Chicago.

1890 Jacob Riis publishes *How the Other Half Lives*, exposing the harsh tenement life of New York immigrants.

1892 Conservationist John Muir founds the Sierra Club.

1893 *McClure's Magazine* founded.

1896 William McKinley (1897–1901) elected president.

1898 The United States easily defeats Spain in the Spanish-American War.

1899 Thorstein Veblen publishes *The Theory of the Leisure Class,* which criticizes turn-of-the-century culture.

1901 Theodore Roosevelt (1901–1909) becomes president after the assassination of William McKinley; Ida B. Wells-Barnett publishes *Lynching and the Excuse for It.*

1902 Writing for *McClure's Magazine*, journalist Ida Tarbell exposes unfair business practices of the Standard Oil Company.

1904 Six of Lincoln Steffens's articles about political corruption are published as *The Shame of Cities.*

1906 Congress passes the American Antiquities Act, allowing the president to establish national historic landmarks and national parks; Upton Sinclair publishes *The Jungle,* exposing unsanitary practices in the meatpacking industry.

Progressivism (1880s–1933)

1909 Congress passes the Payne-Aldrich Tariff.

1910 Progressive Republican House member George W. Norris works to limit the power of the Speaker of the House; Progressive Hiram Johnson is elected governor of California.

1911 U.S. Supreme Court orders the breakup of the Standard Oil Company.

1912 Democrat Woodrow Wilson (1913–1921) is elected president after the Republican Party's support splits between incumbent William Howard Taft (1909–1913) and former president Theodore Roosevelt.

1913 Sixteenth Amendment, permitting the income tax, ratified; Seventeenth Amendment, providing for the direct election of United States senators, also ratified.

1914 World War I (1914–1918) breaks out in Europe.

1916 Jeannette Rankin wins a seat in the House of Representatives, becoming the first woman elected to Congress.

1917 United States enters World War I on the side of the Allies.

1918 World War I ends.

1919 Eighteenth Amendment ratified, beginning era of Prohibition.

1920 Nineteenth Amendment ratified, giving women the right to vote in all elections.

1921 President Warren G. Harding (1921–1923) names former president William Howard Taft Chief Justice of the United States.

1924 Robert La Follette runs for president as a Progressive third-party candidate; Congress passes Child Labor Amendment, but it is not ratified by the states.

1933 Senator George W. Norris secures passage of the Twentieth Amendment, eliminating the "lame duck" session of Congress and thereby making government more responsible to the people; Twenty-first Amendment ratified, repealing the Eighteenth Amendment and ending prohibition.

Preface

The United States was founded on ideas. Those who wrote the U.S. Constitution were influenced by ideas that began in Europe: reason over religion, human rights over the rights of kings, and self-governance over tyranny. Ideas, and the arguments over them, have continued to shape the nation. Of all the ideas that influenced the nation's founding and its growth, 10 are perhaps the most important and are singled out here in an original series–KEY CONCEPTS IN AMERICAN HISTORY. The volumes bring these concepts to life, *Abolitionism, Colonialism, Expansionism, Federalism, Industrialism, Internationalism, Isolationism, Nationalism, Progressivism*, and *Terrorism*.

These books examine the big ideas, major events, and influential individuals that have helped define American history. Each book features three sections. The first is an overview of the concept, its historical context, the debates over the concept, and how it changed the history and growth of the United States. The second is an encyclopedic, A-to-Z treatment of the people, events, issues, and organizations that help to define the "-ism" under review. Here, readers will find detailed facts and vivid histories, along with referrals to other books for more details about the topic.

Interspersed throughout the entries are many high-interest features: "History Speaks" provides excerpts of documents, speeches, and letters from some of the most influential figures in American history. "History Makers" provides brief biographies of key people who dramatically influenced the country. "Then and Now" helps readers connect issues of the nation's past with present-day concerns.

In the third part of each volume, "Viewpoints," readers will find longer primary documents illustrating ideas that reflect a certain point of view of the time. Also included are important government documents and key Supreme Court decisions.

The KEY CONCEPTS series also features "Milestones in. . . ," time lines that will enable readers to quickly sort out how one event led to another, a glossary, and a bibliography for further reading.

People make decisions that determine history, and Americans have generated and refined the ideas that have determined U.S. history. With an understanding of the most important concepts that have shaped our past, readers can gain a better idea of what has shaped our present.

Jennifer L. Weber, Ph.D.
Assistant Professor of History, University of Kansas
General Editor

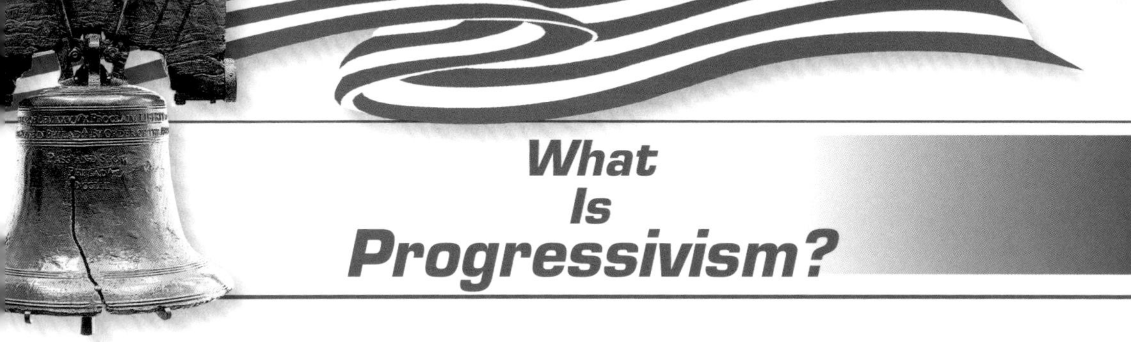

What Is Progressivism?

In American history, the period between the late 1800s and early 1900s is often called the Progressive Era. This was a time of enormous social, political, and economic change that touched every aspect of American life. By the late nineteenth century, after decades of expansion due to the push westward and years of growth due to the Industrial Revolution, the United States had truly become a modern nation.

A hand-tinted photograph from 1912 shows suffragists marching in New York City, demanding the right to vote. Women had been calling for the right to vote since the late 1840s, but not until the ratification of the Nineteenth Amendment in 1920 did women receive the vote across the nation.

THE PROGRESSIVES

Some Americans, however, soon began to notice serious social problems arising from the demands of this new modern society. These Americans, known as **Progressives**, believed that the federal government needed to step in and take control of public life in ways that it had never done before. This practice—of working for social, political, or economic change to improve the lives of people—is called Progressivism. For the first time, Americans demanded that government, including the federal government, act as a means to **reform** society for the better.

Although Progressives mostly came from the **middle class**, they were not just one group of people. Progressives included political leaders, labor leaders, religious leaders, teachers, and journalists. Yet all had basically the same goal—to improve the social and political conditions of the United States and to give more rights to American citizens.

PROGRESSIVES AND BIG BUSINESS

Big business was one of the Progressives' first targets for reform. With the growth of business during the second half of the 1800s, many Americans had become concerned about the increasing power and wealth of **corporations**. Many large corporations had become **monopolies**, or companies that control an entire industry. The railroad industry was an example. Because railroads were then the main means of transportation throughout the country, the companies that ran them were powerful. The Interstate Commerce Act of 1887 made the railroad companies the first American industry to be regulated by the federal government. It was the model for future government regulations of private businesses in the United States.

Another important Progressive reform of big business was the Sherman Antitrust Act of 1890. This was the first act passed by Congress that prohibited **trusts**, or agreements made by groups of companies to fix, or set, prices, thereby ending competition. When fixing prices, companies could agree on charging equally high rates to their customers. The Sherman Antitrust Act authorized the federal government to dissolve trusts. However, it was not until President Theodore Roosevelt's (1901–1909) "trust-busting campaign" of the early 1900s that the Sherman Antitrust Act was really used successfully.

SOCIAL REFORMS

Social reform was another important part of the Progressive movement. In 1890, journalist and photographer Jacob Riis published *How the Other Half Lives*, which depicted in words and pictures the miserable lives of **immigrants** in city **tenements.** The book opened many Americans' eyes to the hidden plight of the poor. Around the same time, social reformers Jane Addams and Ellen Starr established Hull House, a settlement house in Chicago that provided much-needed services to the poor and served as a model for other settlement houses across the country.

Temperance Movement Many social reformers believed that alcoholic beverages were to blame for the worst problems in society, including poverty, unemployment, domestic abuse, and health troubles. These reformers worked to reduce and ultimately ban alcohol's consumption. The temperance movement, which had started in the early 1800s and then lost support, gained new momentum during the Progressive Era, and, because of its increasing pressure on Congress, the movement managed to secure the passage of the Eighteenth Amendment in 1919. This amendment established Prohibition—the banning of the sale, manufacture, and transportation of alcohol for consumption in the United States.

Prohibition was one of the few reforms of the Progressive Era that failed. Instead of reducing alcohol consumption, it merely turned it into an illegal and underground operation. In addition, many Americans felt that Prohibition gave the federal government too much control over people's personal lives. By 1933, the country had had enough of Prohibition and pushed Congress to pass the Twenty-first Amendment, which repealed the Eighteenth Amendment and ended Prohibition.

Suffrage Woman's suffrage, or the right to vote, which was granted by the Nineteenth Amendment in 1920, was another important social reform achieved during the Progressive era. Although the women's rights movement in the United States had actively begun as early as the 1840s, it took nearly 80 years before its ultimate goal was accomplished.

Many leaders of these two movements were also instrumental in passing child-labor laws. With the **Industrial Revolution** came a rise in the number of children working in factories and other businesses. As early as the 1830s, many states had enacted laws restricting or prohibiting the employment of children in factories. However, in rural areas where child labor on farms was common, employment of children in mills and factories was seen as a natural outgrowth. Some Americans even believed that employment actually improved the lives of poor children. Social reformers fought these misconceptions and abuses. Founders of places such as Hull House were instrumental in getting protective legislation enacted on a national level for women and children, laws that included the Federal Children's Bureau in 1912 and the federal child labor law in 1916. The Children's Bureau worked to abolish child labor, promote children's health, and reclaim children who dropped out of school. The Bureau, as well as the 1916 child labor law, laid the foundation for the social legislation of the 1930s.

CONSERVATION OF NATURAL RESOURCES

Conservation, or the protection of natural resources for future generations, was another important movement that grew out of the Progressive Era. By the late 1800s, natural resources in the United States had been greatly used up, especially in the West. Developers had taken over large tracts of forests and grazing land for new homes. Mining companies had destroyed land through wasteful practices. Many Americans had come to believe that there was an endless supply of natural resources in the United States and had no regard for safeguarding or reusing these resources. Progressives, alarmed by this wasteful attitude, called for federal supervision and preservation of the nation's natural riches.

With the support of President Theodore Roosevelt (1901–1909), conservationists accomplished much during the Progressive Era. Roosevelt himself had been greatly influenced by the work of American naturalist John Muir and by Chief of Forestry Gifford Pinchot. In 1905, Roosevelt urged Congress to establish the United States Forest Service to manage government forest lands; Pinchot was appointed as head of the service. By 1909, the Roosevelt administration had set aside 42 million acres (16,996,797 hectares) of land as national forests, 53 national wildlife refuges, and 18 areas of special interest, which included the Grand Canyon. Roosevelt believed that Americans should use natural resources wisely and preserve them for future generations.

MUCKRAKERS

The Progressive movement could not have become so powerful or so well known without the help of **muckrakers,** or investigative reporters, novelists, and critics who exposed acts of corruption and unfairness in American politics and business during the early 1900s. The muckrakers got their name from President Theodore Roosevelt, who in a 1906 speech compared them to a character in John Bunyan's novel *Pilgrim's Progress* (1678), a character who raked muck off the floor. Roosevelt claimed that muckrakers only sought out the muck, or evil, in society. Though Roosevelt was actually an early supporter of the muckrakers, he felt threatened when a muckraking journalist exposed corrupt practices in the U.S. Senate, attacking some of Roosevelt's political allies.

The Jungle Theodore Roosevelt responded positively to another muckraking work, the 1906 novel *The Jungle*, which exposed the terrible and unsanitary working conditions in Chicago's meatpacking plants. After reading *The Jungle*, Roosevelt sent agents to Chicago to determine whether the meatpacking plants were as bad as the novel depicted them and found that they were actually much worse.

By June 1906, Congress had passed the Pure Food and Drug Act, which set federal standards for all packaged food and drugs, and the Meat Inspection Act, which called for federal inspection of all meat-processing plants.

Constitutional Amendments Government reform was also a target of the Progressives. The passage in 1913 of the Sixteenth Amendment to the U.S. Constitution allowed Congress to tax the income of individuals without regard to the population of each state. This allowed for a graduated income tax, or a tax based on what people earned. Progressives felt that it was fairest to ask those who earned the most money to pay the highest tax rates.

The Seventeenth Amendment to the Constitution allowed for the direct election of senators by the people of a state rather than by appointment by the state legislature, as the Constitution had directed. Progressives had argued that state legislatures were often controlled by corrupt leaders who looked out for their own interests and did not represent the best interests of the people. With the passage of the Seventeenth Amendment, all senators would now be directly elected by the people, just as the members of the House of Representatives were.

POLITICS AND PARTIES

In 1908, after serving two terms as president, Theodore Roosevelt encouraged the Republican Party to nominate his close friend, Secretary of War William Howard Taft, to succeed him. When Taft (1909–1913) won the election, Roosevelt assumed that Taft would continue to support his progressive plans. However, Taft and his policies proved to be a disappointment to Roosevelt and other Progressives.

By 1911, progressive Republicans dissatisfied with President Taft's administration formed the National Progressive Republican League, led by Wisconsin senator Robert La Follette. The group supported La Follette for the Republican presidential nomination in 1912, until Theodore Roosevelt decided to run again. Once it became clear that the

Republicans would choose Taft as their nominee, Roosevelt endorsed the formation of a new, progressive party. Later that summer, the newly created Progressive Party officially nominated Theodore Roosevelt as its presidential nominee. After Roosevelt became the party's candidate for president, he said he felt "as strong as a bull moose," which then became the nickname of the party.

Theodore Roosevelt believed that a strong federal government was necessary to regulate industry and protect the working class. His Progressive Party promised several governmental reforms, including the direct election of senators, the setting of minimum-wage standards, the prohibition of child labor, and government regulation of business. It also became the first national political party to support woman suffrage.

Though Roosevelt ultimately lost the election of 1912, he won 27 percent of the popular vote and had taken enough votes away from conservative President Taft to ensure Taft's defeat. The winner of the election was progressive Democrat Woodrow Wilson (1913–1921). Thus, the election was still viewed as a victory for the Progressives.

Most historians consider the Progressive Era to have ended in the 1920s. After World War I (1914–1918), the United States became much more conservative, both socially and politically. After the 1917 Russian Revolution brought the **communists** to power, many Americans, fearing such a revolution at home, did not want the federal government to have as much control over their lives. The election of conservative Republican president Warren Harding (1921–1923) in 1920 was a strong indication that Americans were less supportive of progressive leaders than they had been. Although Robert La Follette ran on the Progressive Party ticket in 1924, he was easily defeated by another conservative Republican, the incumbent president Calvin Coolidge (1923–1929).

Benefits Today Although the Progressive Era of the late 1800s and early 1900s eventually ended, the United States continues to benefit from its legacy.

Election of 1912

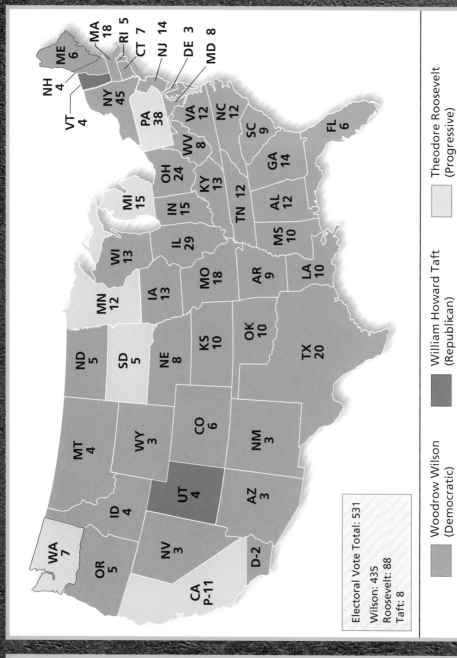

ME 6
NH 4
VT 4
MA 18
RI 5
CT 7
NJ 14
DE 3
MD 8
NY 45
PA 38
VA 12
NC 12
SC 9
FL 6
WV 8
GA 14
OH 24
KY 13
MI 15
IN 15
TN 12
AL 12
MS 10
IL 29
WI 13
AR 9
LA 10
MO 18
MN 12
IA 13
OK 10
KS 10
TX 20
ND 5
SD 5
NE 8
CO 6
NM 3
WY 3
MT 4
UT 4
AZ 3
ID 4
NV 3
WA 7
OR 5
CA P-11
D-2

Electoral Vote Total: 531

Wilson: 435
Roosevelt: 88
Taft: 8

Woodrow Wilson (Democratic)
William Howard Taft (Republican)
Theodore Roosevelt (Progressive)

Note: The coloring found in the states with a split electoral vote does not bear any geographic significance.

© Infobase Publishing

The sharp divisions in the Republican Party helped ensure Democrat Woodrow Wilson's victory in the election of 1912.

Most of the reforms passed during that time are still in effect today, and many have been updated and improved. Future generations have been inspired by the demand for reform in social, political, and economic aspects of society, and other movements, such as the civil rights movement of the 1950s and 1960s, arose out of a similar heightened consciousness to bring change to better the lives of all Americans.

The Progressive Spirit Remains In the twenty-first century, the spirit of Progressivism remains a vital part of the nation's culture. In January 2009, newly elected president Barack Obama (2009–) spoke of the need for change and progress in his historic inaugural address:

> . . . everywhere we look, there is work to be done. The state of the economy calls for action, bold and swift, and we will act—not only to create new jobs, but to lay a new foundation for growth. We will build the roads and bridges, the electric grids and digital lines that feed our commerce and bind us together. We will restore science to its rightful place, and wield technology's wonders to raise health care's quality and lower its cost. We will harness the sun and the winds and the soil to fuel our cars and run our factories. And we will transform our schools and colleges and universities to meet the demands of a new age. All this we can do. And all this we will do.

Further Reading

Eisenach, Eldon J., ed. *The Social and Political Thought of American Progressivism*. Indianapolis, Ind.: Hackett Publishing, 2006.

Flanagan, Maureen A. *America Reformed: Progressives and Progressivisms, 1890s–1920s*. New York: Oxford Books, 2006.

McNeese, Tim. *The Progressive Movement: Advocating Social Change*. New York: Chelsea House, 2007.

Pestritto, Ronald J. *American Progressivism: A Reader.* Lanham, Md.: Lexington Books, 2008.

Progressivism from A to Z

A–C

Addams, Jane (1860–1935)

Influential **social worker** and first American woman to win the Nobel Peace Prize. Born in 1860 in Cedarville, Illinois, to an upper-class family, Addams became the acknowledged leader of social settlement work in the United States. She believed that all classes were entitled to an education and exposure to high culture.

Addams's father, John, was a successful businessman and member of the state **legislature**. Her mother, Sarah, was occupied with both the home life of her large family as well as making meals for the workers in the mills the Addams family owned. Sarah died when Jane was three, and Jane subsequently developed a close relationship with her father. He encouraged her to go to Rockford Female Seminary, an all-women's college that had been attended by two of her sisters.

Jane was an exceptional student and was class president and editor of the school newspaper. In 1881, she graduated first in her class. Jane wanted to study medicine following graduation, much to the dismay of her father. As an upper-class woman, Jane was expected to marry and carry on the duties of a lady. Practicing medicine, it was feared, would make her less desirable as a wife and less interested in taking a husband.

Despite her father's protests, Jane began taking classes in medicine. In 1881, John Addams died, and Jane found herself unable to concentrate on her work. She left school to travel Europe and try to decide what to do with her life. A classmate, Ellen Starr, accompanied her on her travels.

FIRST VISIT TO A SETTLEMENT HOUSE

During a trip to East London, Addams began to develop a sense of empathy for the great poverty she was witnessing. She also saw Toynbee Hall, her first visit to a settlement house, during this trip. A settlement house was like a boardinghouse where educated men and women would settle into poverty-stricken areas of the city. These men and women would then serve as teachers and models for the urban poor, gaining a sense of understanding and empathy for people that they otherwise would never have met.

HULL HOUSE IS FOUNDED

In June 1888, Addams had decided that she was going to set up a settlement house of her own. She sought advice at Toynbee Hall in London, and in January of 1889, after retuning to the United States, Addams and Ellen Starr began searching for a location for their settlement house. The building they found was a mansion on Polk and Halsted streets in Chicago that had once been the home of Charles Hull. The women moved in on September 18, 1889.

In Addams's view, settlement houses were part of a larger movement of social reform. The upper and lower classes were separated by a vast gap in income. Addams felt that this extreme gap was a threat to democracy. As long as the classes held nothing in common, there was nothing holding the country together. They would not support one another's causes because they would always view each other as adversaries. The settlement houses would bring people together, educating both upper- and lower-class participants about the things they had in common.

Hull House strove to introduce its visitors to high, versus popular, culture. Working-class people generally did not develop much of an appreciation for the arts nor have either the finances or opportunity to attend theater. Hull House added an art gallery and music school to its offerings. Multiculturalism was also a large driving force behind Hull House. Addams believed that people should be educated about the cultures of other immigrants. She established Hull House Labor Museum to highlight the lives immigrants led in their country of origin. The location Addams and Starr had chosen put the people of the house in close contact with Russian and Polish Jews, Bohemians, Greeks, Irish, Italians, Germans, Mexicans, and African Americans. As Addams later wrote:

> It seemed to me that Hull-House ought to be able to devise some educational enterprise which should build a bridge between European and American experiences in such ways as to give them both more meaning and a sense of relation. I meditated that perhaps the power to see life as a whole is more needed in the immigrant quarter of a large city than anywhere else, and that the lack of this power is the most fruitful source of misunderstanding between European immigrants and their children, as it is between them and their American neighbors; and why should that chasm between fathers and sons, yawning at the feet of each generation, be made so unnecessarily cruel and impassable to these bewildered immigrants?

Addams also set up adult education classes at night and ran a coffeehouse to give visitors a place to relax and meet one another.

Addams also was connected to the academic world, which took great interest in her work. She was a member of the Chicago School of Sociology and a colleague of philosopher and psychologist George H. Mead. Together, they worked to reform child labor laws and increase women's rights. Addams's work was motivated by **feminism** and **idealism**, but she took a realistic approach to change. She worked to change people's lives in substantial ways, and these changes were proof that her ideas were valid. The bonds formed at Hull House helped create the Juvenile Protection Agency and push child labor laws through the Illinois legislature in 1893. In 1916, the federal government passed similar laws.

PEACE MOVEMENTS

As an activist, Addams put considerable effort into creating a peace movement. In response to World War I (1914–1918), Addams organized the Women's Peace Party. Their first meeting was in Washington, D.C. Women from a variety of backgrounds met to call for an end to the war and for cultural changes that would make war unnecessary. The women generally agreed that as the "mothers of humanity" they had a duty to try to put a stop to the slaughter of the war. Toward that end, a number of women from many of the nations involved in the conflict met at The Hague in the Netherlands at the International Congress of Women in 1915. The Congress eventually became the Women's International League for Peace and Freedom. At the time, Addams was regarded as dangerous and **unpatriotic** for speaking out against the war. Later, in 1931, her work earned her the Nobel Peace Prize. Jane Addams died on May 21, 1935, in Chicago.

See also: Child Labor; Hull House; Social Justice.

Further Reading

Berson, Robin. *Jane Addams: A Biography.* Westport, Conn.: Greenwood Press, 2004.

Linn, James Weber. *Jane Addams: A Biography.* Champaign: University of Illinois Press, 2000.

Anthony, Susan B. (1820–1906)

Women's rights activist and writer. Anthony wrote and worked tirelessly on behalf of **suffrage** and became the driving force behind the National Woman Suffrage Association.

Susan B. Anthony was born on February 15, 1820, in Adams, Massachusetts, to Daniel Anthony and Lucy Read. She was one of seven children. Anthony was a quick learner. She could read and write when she was three. She and her family were **Quakers**, who encouraged a strong moral character and active political life. Her father was an **abolitionist**, and her mother attended conventions on women's rights.

In 1826, Anthony's family moved to Battenville, New York. Susan was sent to school but was quickly removed because the schoolmaster would not teach her the same lessons as he was teaching the boys. Anthony was home-schooled by her father instead. In 1837, she was sent to a Quaker boarding school near Philadelphia called Deborah Moulson's Female Seminary, a school for young women. That same year, her family suffered great financial loss and bankruptcy in the Panic of 1837, a nationwide financial crisis. Many banks went out of business, and many people lost their savings.

Heavily in debt, the Anthony family sold everything they had and moved to Hardscrabble, New

York, now called Center Falls. In 1839, Susan got a job teaching at a Quaker school in New Rochelle, New York. These early jobs instilled in her an indignation that would fuel her fight for women's rights. As a teacher, she earned one-fourth the amount that a man earned for the same job.

This 1900 photograph, enhanced with oil paint, depicts women's rights activist Susan B. Anthony. Committed to women's right to vote, Anthony voted in the 1872 presidential election, for which she was arrested and fined. Throughout her career, she gave between 75 and 100 speeches a year in support of women's rights.

WORKING FOR SOCIAL JUSTICE

In 1849, Anthony left her teaching job and moved to Rochester, New York. There she came into contact with leading abolitionists of the day, whose influence encouraged her into active political life. She also joined the temperance movement, a movement to discourage the use of alcohol, which eventually led to Prohibition.

While in Rochester, Anthony found her faith in Quakerism waning. She attended a Unitarian church, but became increasingly critical of all organized religion over time.

In 1851, Anthony was introduced to Elizabeth Cady Stanton and Amelia Bloomer, two of the country's most prominent feminists and women's suffragists. Stanton had organized the Seneca Falls Convention three years earlier, kicking off the organized effort to seek equal rights for women. A second convention was held in Syracuse, New York in 1852.

Anthony traveled the country giving speeches in support of the temperance movement and women's rights, and she was gaining fame in the newspapers, which often criticized her. In 1860, she became part of the abolitionist movement and helped found the National Women's Loyal League, which urged **emancipation** of the slaves. When the Fourteenth Amendment to guarantee equal rights to blacks (which was **ratified** in 1868) was being discussed,

Anthony campaigned to have women included in the amendment. Her campaign, however, failed.

In 1868, she and Elizabeth Cady Stanton founded the *Revolution*, a newspaper supporting equal rights and suffrage for both women and blacks. In 1869, Anthony and Stanton organized the National Woman Suffrage Association (NWSA), and Anthony began to tour the country again, giving speeches.

WORKING FOR WOMEN'S RIGHT TO VOTE

In 1872, she protested the lack of women's suffrage by voting for president. She was arrested and convicted in a **kangaroo court** trial–a biased trial in which the outcome is usually already known. The judge had written his decision before the case was even presented.

Anthony had hoped that the courts would rule that the wording of the Fourteenth Amendment applied to women, thus bypassing the legislature that refused to extend equal rights to women. The first section of the Fourteenth Amendment states:

> All persons born or naturalized in the United States, and subject to the jurisdiction thereof, are citizens of the United States and of the State wherein they reside. No State shall make or enforce any law which shall abridge the privileges or immunities of citizens of the United States; nor shall any State deprive any person of life, liberty, or property, without due process of law; nor deny to any person within its jurisdiction the equal protection of the laws.

It was the lack of gender-specific terms in this section that Anthony hoped would support her cause.

Once convicted, Anthony was fined, but she refused to pay the fine for the rest of her life. The trial gained national attention, however, and Anthony's detractors had unwittingly given her a stage on which to present her case for women's suffrage. She had the **transcript** of the trial printed and distributed, and she traveled the country to recount her treatment.

Anthony continued to work for women's suffrage throughout her life. In 1890, she was instrumental in bringing the NWSA and the American Woman Suffrage Association together to form the National American Woman Suffrage Association. The new, larger organization was more moderate than some of Anthony's compatriots would have liked. Yet Anthony maintained that moderate views were more likely to achieve change than radical ones.

She believed that women's suffrage was inevitable and gave her last speech in February 1906. She declared that "Failure is impossible!" Susan B. Anthony died on March 13, 1906. The right to vote was extended to women with ratification of the Nineteenth Amendment in 1920.

See also: Prohibition; Stanton, Elizabeth Cady; Suffragists; Temperance Movement; Woman Suffrage.

FURTHER READING

Anthony, Susan B. *The Trial of Susan B. Anthony.* Amherst, N.Y.: Humanity Books, 2003.

Barry, Kathleen. *Susan B. Anthony: A Biography of a Singular Feminist.* Bloomington, Ind.: 1st Books Library, 2000.

Stalcup, Brenda, ed. *Susan B. Anthony.* Farmington Hills, Mich.: Greenhaven Press, 2001.

Todd, Anne M. *Susan B. Anthony.* New York: Chelsea House, 2009.

Bull Moose Party

Another name for the short-lived **reform** party known as the Progressive Party, established in 1912. When former president Theodore Roosevelt (1901–1909) became the Progressive Party candidate for president in 1912, he said he felt "as strong as a bull moose." Thus, the party became known as the Bull Moose Party.

The Bull Moose Party was formed in 1912 because of long-term troubles within the Republican Party, the major American political party that had been established in 1854. During his time as president, between 1901 and 1909, Theodore Roosevelt became known as a great promoter of **progressive** reform. He supported organized labor, government regulation of business, consumer protection, and conservation. Because many conservatives in the Republican Party supported big business, they clashed with Roosevelt's progressive ideals.

After nearly two terms as president, Theodore Roosevelt promised not to run for a third term. Instead he encouraged the Republican Party to nominate his close friend, Secretary of War William Howard Taft (1909–1913), to succeed him. When Taft won the election, Roosevelt assumed that Taft would continue to support his progressive plans. However, Taft, who stuck closely to the law and lacked Roosevelt's sharp political skills, proved to be a disappointment to Roosevelt and other Progressives. Taft supported the Payne Aldrich Tariff Act, which lowered U.S. taxes on goods entering the country, but not as much as Progressives had hoped. Unlike Roosevelt, Taft never publicly attacked big business, even though he supported government regulation. This conservative stance angered Roosevelt and further divided the Republican Party.

PROGRESSIVE REPUBLICANS ORGANIZE

By 1911, progressive Republicans dissatisfied with President Taft's administration formed the National Progressive Republican League, which was led by Wisconsin senator Robert La Follette (1855–1925). The group supported Senator La Follette for the Republican presidential nomination in 1912, until former president Theodore Roosevelt decided to run again. Once it was clear at the Republican National Convention in June that Taft would be chosen as the Republican nominee, Roosevelt asked his followers to leave the convention hall and endorsed the formation of a new, progressive party. Later that summer, the newly created Progressive Party, or Bull Moose Party, officially nominated Theodore Roosevelt as its presidential nominee and California senator Hiram Johnson for vice president.

The platform of the Progressive Party declared that:

> Unhampered by tradition, uncorrupted by power, undismayed by the magnitude of the task, the new party offers itself as the instrument of the people to sweep away old abuses, to build a new and nobler commonwealth.

The Progressive Party promised various governmental reforms, including the direct popular election of senators, minimum wage standards, prohibition of child labor, and government regulation of business. It also became the first national political party to support woman **suffrage**, or the right to vote.

ELECTION OF 1912

The winner of the 1912 presidential election was the Democratic candidate, Woodrow Wilson (1913–1921), who was serving as the governor of New Jersey. Wilson, however, had received less than half of the popular votes. Roosevelt and his Bull Moose Party had taken votes away from the Republicans. Because Wilson also supported progressive reforms, the election was still considered a victory for the Progressives. The Progressive Party continued to remain active for years but did not nominate a presidential candidate again until 1924, when Senator Robert La Follette ran for president.

See also: Election of 1912; Johnson, Hiram; La Follette, Robert; Payne-Aldrich Tariff Act; Progressive Party; Roosevelt, Theodore; Taft, William Howard; Wilson, Woodrow.

Further Reading

Gould, Lewis L., ed. *Bull Moose on the Stump: The 1912 Campaign Speeches of Theodore Roosevelt*. Lawrence: University of Kansas Press, 2008.

Child Labor

The practice of employing children under age 18 in factories, mines, and other businesses for long hours and at wages less than adults might earn. By the early part of the twentieth century, many children in the United States worked in mines, factories, textiles, and canneries. Many also worked as newsboys, messengers, and peddlers. Often factory owners preferred to hire children because they were considered easier to manage, cheaper, and less likely to strike.

Working conditions for children were, in general, worse in the cotton fields and mills of the South than elsewhere, but in the textile factories of New England and in the garment **sweatshops** of New York City, children worked long hours at low pay and under horrible conditions. Factories and mills were not well ventilated—they were hot in the summer and cold in the winter. Work breaks were unheard of, and factory doors were often locked. Rats and insects were common.

LABOR LAWS AND CHILDREN

As early as the 1830s, many states had enacted laws restricting or prohibiting the employment of young children in factories. Yet in rural

Children working in a glass-making factory pose for this 1908 photograph by Lewis W. Hine, who documented the frightful working conditions of children in the United States. Often, children as young as five began working in factories.

communities, where children regularly worked on farms, the employment of children in mills and factories did not concern most people. Many Americans also believed that sending poor children to work actually helped poor families and the community at large.

CALL FOR LEGISLATION

Social workers, such as Jane Addams, realized that these miserable conditions led to illness and early death. **Progressive** reformers called for legislation to improve working conditions, especially for children. In spite of opposition from big business, individual states began to pass various types of labor legislation, including safety laws, as well as requiring school attendance and limiting the number of hours children were allowed to work.

As labor laws varied from state to state, employers in those states with the strictest laws suffered because competitors in other states could produce goods cheaper than they could. In general, however, local child-labor laws were often ignored. Also, in many cases the laws did not apply to immigrants, and therefore the children of **immigrants** were forced to work the longest hours for little pay.

The Proposed Child Labor Amendment

The Child Labor Amendment was a proposed amendment to the U.S. Constitution introduced to Congress by Republican Ohio congressman Israel Moore Foster in 1924. The amendment passed the U.S. House of Representatives on April 26, 1924. It was then passed by the Senate on June 2, 1924. The proposed amendment was next submitted to the various state legislatures for **ratification**.

Although most Americans supported child labor laws, the Child Labor Amendment was strongly debated throughout the states. Many opponents feared that the passage of a national Child Labor Amendment would forbid children to do work on their own family farms, which was a very common practice in rural areas. They argued that the amendment would give Congress power over what should be a family decision. Therefore, they felt that the issue should be addressed by local governments and not the federal government. Yet, supporters of the amendment believed that the country as a whole needed to protect children, who would later become its future citizens.

Republican presidents Calvin Coolidge and Herbert Hoover supported the Child Labor Amendment, as did both major political parties. Most social reform groups campaigned for the amendment. However, other organizations that represented big businesses, as well as various groups that disliked government regulation, spoke out against the amendment. Ultimately, it was ratified by the legislatures of only 28 states, the last in 1937, but not the three-fourths majority needed to make it a law. In 1938, the Fair Labor Standards Act put child labor under the control of the Department of Labor, making the Child Labor Amendment no longer necessary. The unratified amendment was composed of two sections:

> Section 1. The Congress shall have power to limit, regulate, and prohibit the labor of persons under eighteen years of age.
>
> Section 2. The power of the several States is unimpaired by this article except that the operation of State laws shall be suspended to the extent necessary to give effect to legislation enacted by the Congress.

Soon, reformers called for federal action to regulate child labor.

SOME SUCCESSES

In 1904, the National Child Labor Committee was formed to protect the rights of working children. Four years later, the committee hired American sociologist and photographer Lewis Hine to investigate and document child labor around the country. Hine traveled thousands of miles across the United States, taking pictures of children working in factories. Many factory owners refused to let Hine take photographs of their child workers. Sometimes Hine posed as a fire inspector and secretly took pictures.

Hine's photographs were published in two collections called *Child Labor in the Carolinas* and *Day Laborers Before Their Time.* Hine believed that if more Americans saw the terrible working conditions of child factory workers, they would push for child labor reform. Hine also gave public lectures about child labor. He told one audience, "Perhaps you are weary of child labor pictures. Well, so are the rest of us, but we propose to make you and the whole country so sick and tired of the whole business that when the time for action comes, child labor pictures will be records of the past."

A major step forward in child labor reform occurred in 1912 with the founding of the Children's Bureau, which is today a part of the Department of Health and Human Services. Under the direction of Julia Lathrop, the bureau collected information and offered suggestions to improve the lot of children. In 1916, Congress passed the Keating-Owen Law, which prohibited the interstate shipment of goods made by children. This law, however, was declared unconstitutional by the U.S. Supreme Court.

In 1924, Congress passed a proposed Child Labor Amendment to the Constitution, which granted Congress the power to regulate the labor of children under the age of 18. Though the amendment passed in both the House and Senate, it failed to be **ratified** by a sufficient number of states. Opponents to the amendment argued that children would become responsible to the government and not to their own parents. In the 1930s and 1940s, various acts of President Franklin D. Roosevelt (1933–1945), under what was known as his New Deal, finally addressed the issue of child labor.

See also: Social Justice.

FURTHER READING

Bartoletti, Susan Campbell. *Kids on Strike!* New York: Sandpiper, 2003.

Freedman, Russell. *Kids at Work: Lewis Hine and the Crusade Against Child Labor.* Boston: Clarion Books, 1994.

Goldberg, Vicki. *Lewis W. Hine: Children at Work.* New York: Prestel Publishing, 1999.

Conservation

A key goal of the Progressive movement, requiring the preservation of the nation's natural resources for the use and enjoyment of future generations. Since colonial days, the American people had been careless with the nation's seemingly endless resources. During the presidencies of Benjamin Harrison (1889–1893), Grover Cleveland (1983–1897), and William McKinley (1897–1901), some efforts had been made to preserve **timberland**. In general, however, government policies had not favored **conservationists**, or people who encourage the protection of natural resources.

ROOSEVELT AND THE CONSERVATION MOVEMENT

President Theodore Roosevelt (1901–1909), a **Progressive** and a hearty outdoorsman, had a deep interest in nature. Soon after assuming the presidency, upon the assassination of President McKinley, Roosevelt began furthering the conservationists' cause. He believed that it was:

> Entirely in our power as a nation to preserve large tracts of wilderness, which are valueless for agricultural purposes and unfit for settlement, as playgrounds for rich and poor alike, and to preserve the game so that it shall continue to exist for the benefit of all lovers of nature, and to give

The rugged peaks of the Grand Teton Mountains dominate the view of tourists as they drive though Grand Teton National Park. Located in Wyoming, the park, which is a legacy of the conservation movement of the early 1900s, covers 484 square miles (1,250 sq. km) of land and water.

> reasonable opportunities for the exercise of the skill of the hunter, whether he is or is not a man of means. But this end can only be achieved by wise laws and by a resolute enforcement of the laws. Lack of such legislation and administration will result in harm to all of us, but most of all in harm to the nature lover who does not possess vast wealth.

Roosevelt continued his efforts throughout his seven years in office.

LEADING THE MOVEMENT

Another leader of the conservation movement was Gifford Pinchot, a politician who had studied forestry and was dedicated to conservation. In 1898, he was appointed chief of the United States Forest Service. In this role, he worked tirelessly and built the Forest Service into a major force for conservation. Pinchot and Roosevelt shared many of the same views about the conservation movement, and many of Roosevelt's programs were suggested by Pinchot.

The first important legislation related to conservation was the Newlands Act (1902). This law granted the federal government power to construct dams, reservoirs, and irrigation projects throughout the nation. The full name of the act is *An Act Appropriating the receipts from the sale and disposal of public lands in certain States and Territories to the construction of irrigation works for the reclamation of arid lands.* This law greatly expanded the power of the federal government over public lands. Its key provisions included the following:

- Section 1 identified the 16 states and territories to be included in the project: Arizona, California, Colorado, Idaho, Kansas, Montana, Nebraska, Nevada, New Mexico, North Dakota, Oklahoma, Oregon, South Dakota, Utah, Washington, and Wyoming. It required fees from sales of western land be set aside for a reclamation fund for the development of water resources, and it required the Treasury Department to fund conservation education under certain conditions.
- Section 2 authorized the secretary of the interior to determine the reclamation projects.
- Section 3 required the secretary of the interior to withdraw all such land from public entry.
- Section 4 authorized the secretary of the interior to enter into contracts for the various water projects.
- Section 5 set requirements for those using the water. Among these were that half of the land must be used for agriculture; the user must pay apportioned charges for the water; the user cannot use more than the apportioned water; the user cannot sell water to one neighbor or any water to a nonresident; and the user must pay apportioned charges annually.
- Section 6 authorized the secretary of the interior to use the reclamation fund for all works constructed under the act.
- Section 7 gave the secretary of the interior the power of **eminent domain** for construction projects.

- Section 8 required the secretary of the interior to conform to state laws.
- Section 9 required the secretary of the interior to expend monies generated by each state within that state as much as is possible.
- Section 10 authorized the secretary of the interior to make such rules and regulations as is necessary to carry out the act.

Much of the western United States could not have been settled without the water provided by the act. Today, for example, the more than 600 dams on waterways throughout the U.S. West provide irrigation for about 10 million acres (40,000 sq. km.) of farmland, providing about 60 percent of the nation's vegetables and 25 percent of its fruits and nuts. In addition, although not envisioned by the act, western dams support 58 power plants, producing 40 billion kilowatt hours of electricity annually.

Lawmakers built other laws upon the foundation established by the Newlands Act. During his presidency,

The Conservation Movement

The modern conservation movement in the United States dates from the early years of the nineteenth century. The efforts of leaders such as President Theodore Roosevelt, conservationist Gifford Pinchot, and naturalist John Muir laid the foundation upon which today's environmentalist movement was built.

Pollution of the air, land, and water remains a major problem in the twenty-first century. Every nation faces the consequences of global warming and challenges of environmental issues, including an ever-increasing population, a decrease in natural resources, the lack of clean water, and energy shortages. Through the efforts of world leaders and a variety of global organizations, however, the public's awareness of the need to make difficult, but responsible, choices to conserve our resources is rapidly growing.

Today, for example, the United Nations Environment Programme (UNEP), an organization within the United Nations (UN), has taken a key role in global conservation. This is its mission:

> To provide leadership and encourage partnership in caring for the environment by inspiring, informing, and enabling nations and peoples to improve their quality of life without compromising that of future generations.

In addition, a new generation of world leaders is making environmental issues an essential part of their nations' policies. As President Barack Obama (2009–) noted in his inaugural address on January 20, 2009:

> We will restore science to its rightful place, and wield technology's wonders to raise health care's quality and lower its cost. We will harness the sun and the winds and the soil to fuel our cars and run our factories. And we will transform our schools and colleges and universities to meet the demands of a new age. All this we can do. And all this we will do.

Theodore Roosevelt set aside almost 150 million acres (60,702,846.3 hectares) of timberland as a forest reserve. He also created five national parks. In 1908, Roosevelt held a national conference on conservation. Attended by state and federal officials, as well as by private citizens, the meeting helped sway public opinion in favor of conservation. Soon, 41 states set up conservation commissions to preserve natural resources within their borders.

OPPOSITION TO CONSERVATION

The conservation policies of Roosevelt and Pinchot met severe opposition from several sources. For example, the electric power industry opposed the government's dam-building program because the dams took potential business and revenue away from the electric companies. In addition, the coal and lumber companies wanted to take over the government's land reserve so they could harvest the lands' resources.

The conflict between the conservationists and their opponents came to a head in 1909. During William Howard Taft's administration (1909–1913), several of the government's coal-reserve lands and waterpower sites were turned over to private businesses, an action for which Gifford Pinchot criticized the secretary of the interior, Richard Ballinger. Taft then fired Pinchot, who was still in charge of the Forest Service. Ultimately, President Taft's image was severely damaged by these anti-conservationist actions.

See also: Roosevelt, Theodore.

Further Reading

Gore, Al. *An Inconvenient Truth: The Crisis of Global Warming*. New York: Viking Juvenile, 2007.

Greenland, Paul R., and Annamarie L. Sheldon. *Career Opportunities in Conservation and the Environment*. New York: Checkmark Books, 2007.

Harmon, Daniel E. *Al Gore and Global Warming*. New York: Rosen Publishing, 2008.

Miller, Char. *Gifford Pinchot and the Making of Modern Environmentalism*. Washington, D.C.: Island Press, 2004.

Steen, Harold K. *The U.S. Forest Service: A History*. Seattle: University of Washington Press, 2004.

E–F

Eighteenth Amendment (1919)

Amendment to the U.S. Constitution that prohibited the manufacture, sale, or transportation of liquor within the United States and its **territories**. During the early nineteenth century, many citizens became convinced that Americans were living a sinful life. These people, among them a variety of religious reformers, feared that God would no longer bless the United States. In addition, they also believed that these sinners posed a threat to America's democratic political system and that the nation needed solid, upstanding citizens who did not engage in immoral acts.

RISE OF THE MOVEMENT

Because of the desire to improve social and political conditions in the United States, many people became involved in **reform** movements during the mid-1800s, especially the temperance movement. Temperance supporters encouraged Americans to reduce the amount of alcohol that they consumed. Ideally, they felt, all Americans would give up alcohol entirely, but most temperance advocates were willing to settle for reduced consumption.

The largest organization established to advocate temperance was the American Temperance Society. By the mid-1830s, more than 200,000 people belonged to this organization. The American Temperance Society published pamphlets and hired speakers to inform the public about the negative effects of alcohol upon people and society.

Thus, the movement leading up to national Prohibition was the result of almost a century-long, broad-based temperance crusade. Voluntary

Outlawing Alcohol

Passed at the height of the Progressive Era, the Eighteenth Amendment prohibited the use, manufacture, or sale of intoxicating liquor in the United States and its territories. Prohibition proved unpopular with the vast majority of the American public, however, and created a demand for "bootleg," or illegal, alcohol. As a result, during the 1920s and early 1930s, criminal and gang activity related to bootleg liquor increased significantly. The Eighteenth Amendment was repealed by the Twenty-first Amendment in 1933.

Section 1. After one year from the ratification of this article the manufacture, sale, or transportation of intoxicating liquors within, the importation thereof into, or the exportation thereof from the United States and all territory subject to the jurisdiction thereof for beverage purposes is hereby prohibited.

Section 2. The Congress and the several States shall have concurrent power to enforce this article by appropriate legislation.

Section 3. This article shall be inoperative unless it shall have been ratified as an amendment to the Constitution by the legislatures of the several States, as provided in the Constitution, within seven years from the date of the submission hereof to the States by the Congress.

abstinence campaigns, resulting from the efforts of the American Temperance Society and other such groups, successfully reduced American alcohol consumption. After the Civil War (1861–1865), temperance supporters sought legal bans on liquor to extend the benefits of abstinence, or refraining from any consumption of alcohol.

During the 1850s, 12 states briefly adopted prohibition laws. From about the 1880s until World War I (1914–1918), local and statewide prohibition laws spread. Encouraged by this success, a combination of church groups, feminists, social and political reformers, and business leaders, all of whom believed in the benefits of a "dry" society, began calling for a total, permanent, national solution—constitutional Prohibition.

These various groups pressured Congress, which passed the proposed Eighteenth Amendment by December 18, 1917. It was **ratified** on January 29, 1919, having been approved by 36 states. It went into effect one year later, on January 29, 1920.

PROHIBITION ENDS

Many temperance advocates believed that the struggle was over with Prohibition, causing many of these people to stop participating in anti-alcohol organizations. Prominent financial backers withdrew their support as well. Because of this declining support, anti-temperance supporters were able to introduce in 1933 the Twenty-first Amendment to the U.S. Constitution. That same year, a sufficient number of state-ratifying conventions approved the amendment, ending Prohibition.

See also: Prohibition; Temperance Movement.

Further Reading

Lieurance, Suzanne. *The Prohibition Era in American History.* Berkeley Heights, N.J.: Enslow Publishers, 2003.

Lucas, Eileen. *The Eighteenth and Twenty-First Amendments: Alcohol–Prohibition and Repeal.* Berkeley Heights, N.J.: Enslow Publishers, 1998.

Election of 1912

Presidential election in which Democrat Woodrow Wilson (1913–1921) was elected the 28th president of the United States. During the election of 1912, the newly created Progressive Party nominated its own candidate for president, former president Theodore Roosevelt (1901–1909).

Roosevelt ran as a strong **third-party candidate** against the Democratic and Republican candidates. The campaign itself raised important issues facing the United States at the time, including the future of the economy and the relationship between the federal government and American citizens.

THE CANDIDATES

The Republican candidate in the election of 1912 was the **incumbent**, President William Howard Taft (1909–1913), running for a second term. In the previous election, President Roosevelt had encouraged the Republican Party to nominate Taft, his secretary of war. Yet, as president,

Taft proved to be a disappointment to Roosevelt and other **Progressives** in the Republican Party. Though Taft supported many of Roosevelt's progressive reforms, he did not aggressively go after big business as Roosevelt had done. Taft also supported the Payne-Aldrich Tariff Act, which lowered U.S. taxes on goods entering the country, but not as much as Progressives had hoped. Taft's conservative approach to the presidency had caused a split within the Republican Party between the **conservatives** and the Progressives.

In protest, by 1911, progressive Republicans had formed the National Progressive Republican League, led by Wisconsin senator Robert La Follette. As the 1912 election campaign began, the National Progressive Republican League refused to support Taft as a candidate and instead supported Senator La Follette for the Republican presidential nomination. Yet once it became clear that Taft would be chosen as the Republican nominee, former president Theodore Roosevelt endorsed the formation of a new, progressive party and decided to enter the presidential race himself. Later that summer, the newly created Progressive Party, or Bull Moose Party, officially nominated Theodore Roosevelt as its presidential nominee and California senator Hiram Johnson for vice president.

The Progressive Party promised various governmental reforms, including the direct popular election of senators, minimum wage standards, prohibition of child labor, and government regulation of business. It also became the first national political party to support woman **suffrage**, or the right to vote.

DEMOCRATIC CANDIDATE

Governor Woodrow Wilson of New Jersey was the Democratic candidate for the election of 1912. Like Roosevelt, Wilson was a Progressive, but the two candidates differed on some important points. Wilson wanted to limit the power of government, and he opposed some progressive reforms that Roosevelt supported, including workers' compensation and a minimum wage. He also disagreed with Roosevelt on how certain reforms should be implemented. Whereas Roosevelt wanted to regulate trusts, or big business monopolies, Wilson wanted to eliminate them entirely. On the issue of woman suffrage, which was part of the Progressive Party's platform, Wilson believed that the issue should be decided by each state and not by the federal government. During his campaign, Wilson carefully built a platform that would attract people who supported reform, but he was also able to appeal to the traditional Democratic voters in the South and Northeast. The Democratic platform declared:

> We direct attention to the fact that the Democratic party's demand for a return to the rule of the people expressed in the national platform four years ago, has now become the accepted doctrine of a large majority of the electors. We again remind the country that only by a larger exercise of the reserved power of the people can they protect themselves from the misuse of

> delegated power and the usurpation of government instrumentalities by special interests. . . . The Democratic party offers itself to the country as an agency through which the complete overthrow and extirpation of corruption, fraud, and machine rule in American politics can be effected.

SOCIALIST CANDIDATE

The fourth candidate in the election of 1912 was Eugene V. Debs, running as a **Socialist Party** candidate for the fourth election in a row. Debs believed that both major parties (the Democrats and the Republicans) were not serving the interests of American workers and therefore he took a more radical view, believing that **socialism** was the only answer. Debs supported many progressive reforms, including woman suffrage and child labor reform, but he was mostly concerned with worker rights and supported the right to form unions and to strike.

In part, the 1912 Socialist Party platform stated:

> The Socialist party declares that the **capitalist system** has outgrown its historical function, and has become utterly incapable of meeting the problems now confronting society. We denounce this outgrown system as incompetent and corrupt and the source of unspeakable misery and suffering to the whole working class. . . .
>
> **Working Program**
>
> As measures calculated to strengthen the working class in its fight for the realization of its ultimate aim, the co-operative commonwealth, and to increase its power against capitalist oppression, we advocate and pledge ourselves and our elected officers to the following program:
>
> **Collective Ownership**
>
> 1. The collective ownership and democratic management of railroads, wire and wireless telegraphs and telephones, express service, steamboat lines, and all other social means of transportation and communication and of all large scale industries.
> 2. The immediate acquirement by the municipalities, the states or the federal government of all grain elevators, stock yards, storage warehouses, and other distributing agencies, in order to reduce the present extortionate cost of living. . . .
>
> **Political Demands**
>
> 1. The absolute freedom of press, speech and assemblage.
> 2. The adoption of a graduated income tax and the extension of inheritance taxes, graduated in proportion to the value of the estate and to nearness of kin—the proceeds of these taxes to be employed in the socialization of industry.
> 3. The abolition of the monopoly ownership of patents and

the substitution of collective ownership, with direct rewards to inventors by premiums or royalties.

4. Unrestricted and equal suffrage for men and women.

As candidates, Taft appealed most to conservatives and big business owners, and Debs was popular with farmers in the Midwest and urban workers in the East. Each of these men represented extremes in American society. As moderate social progressives, however, both Wilson and Roosevelt tried to win the voters in the middle.

THE RESULTS

Democrat Woodrow Wilson won the election of 1912, but he received only 42 percent of the popular vote. Roosevelt won 27 percent of the popular vote, even more than Taft's 23 percent. In the end, many people in the labor movement supported Wilson over Eugene Debs, who won only 6 percent of the popular vote.

Though Roosevelt did not win the election for the Progressive Party, he took enough votes away from Taft to ensure that Taft would lose. Also, because three-fourths of American voters had chosen either Wilson or Roosevelt, the election of 1912 was still seen as a victory for the Progressives.

See also: Bull Moose Party; Progressive Party; Roosevelt, Theodore; Taft, William Howard; Wilson, Woodrow.

Further Reading

Brands, H.W. *Woodrow Wilson.* New York: Times Books, 2003.

Chace, James. *1912: Wilson, Roosevelt, Taft and Debs—The Election That Changed the Country.* New York: Simon & Schuster, 2005.

Food and Drug Act, Pure (1906)

Landmark law, passed in 1906, that was designed to prevent the manufacture, sale, or transportation of misbranded or poisonous food, drugs, medicines, and liquors. In addition, the Meat Inspection Act, also passed in 1906, was the first law that provided for federal inspection of all meats to travel in interstate commerce. The law also created the Food and Drug Administration (FDA), which continues to monitor the safety of foods and drugs today.

CALL FOR ACTION

For much of its early history, the United States did not recognize the need for a national food and drug law. Since colonial times, a variety of state laws had been enacted mostly to serve the needs of trade. These state laws set standards of weight and measure and provided for inspections of exports like salt meats, fish, and flour, but these laws were mostly to promote foreign sales of American goods.

By the late 1800s, the change from an agricultural to an industrial country made it necessary to provide the growing populations in cities with food from distant areas. However, sanitation conditions were extremely poor. Ice was usually the only means of refrigeration. Milk did not undergo pasteurization, which is a process that sterilizes milk at high temperatures to kill bacteria. Cows were not tested for diseases such as tuberculosis. New advances in technology meant that chemicals could be used to heighten color, modify flavor, and deter spoilage in canned goods. Yet the use of chemical preservatives and toxic dyes in food was mostly uncontrolled.

At the same time, thousands of "patent" medicines claiming to cure every possible disease or ailment were sold. Some medicines contained harmless ingredients that did not cure anything, but some contained high levels of drugs, including opium and morphine. Labels did not list ingredients, and there were no warning labels.

Veterans of the Spanish-American War (1898) complained bitterly about the spoiled and wormy food they had been issued in army camps in the United States as well as in Cuba. Other Americans criticized the contaminated and even poisonous food and drugs offered for sale and the incredible and often false claims made about them.

The investigative American journalist and novelist Upton Sinclair, as well as other journalists known as muckrakers, wrote of the terrible conditions in the food and drug industries, the filthy environments, the butchering of diseased cattle and hogs, and the sale of spoiled foods and harmful drugs. Government investigation confirmed these horrible stories. President Theodore Roosevelt (1901–1909) became involved in the issue and called for legislative action.

The Pure Food and Drug Act of 1906 forbade "the manufacture, sale, or transportation of adulterated or misbranded or poisonous or deleterious foods, drugs, medicines, and liquors, and for regulating traffic therein, and for other purposes." It also required that products be labeled correctly. Products found to be unsafe could be seized and condemned, and people selling these products could be fined and jailed. The law sought to protect the consumer from being deceived or harmed, based on the belief that the average person would avoid risks if labeling made him or her aware of these risks.

NEW REGULATIONS

Despite the obvious need for a change, for some type of control or regulation, the bills to clean up the food and drug industries were hotly debated, strongly opposed, and, after their passage, often evaded. However, in the late 1910s, with the active and devoted leadership of Dr. Harvey Wiley, a chemist and administrator in the United States Department of Agriculture, Americans finally began to receive fewer harmful drugs and less contaminated and dirty food. The Pure Food and Drug Act was amended in 1912, 1913, and 1919. Then, in 1938, Congress enacted the more comprehensive Food, Drug, and Cosmetic Act that superseded the terms of the Pure Food and Drug Act of 1906.

See also: Muckrakers; Roosevelt, Theodore; Sinclair, Upton.

FURTHER READING

Young, James Harvey. *Pure Food: Securing the Federal Food and Drug Act of 1906.* Princeton, N.J.: Princeton, University Press, 1998.

Hull House

Settlement house cofounded by social reformers Jane Addams (1860–1935) and Ellen Starr (1859–1940) in Chicago in 1889. Settlement houses were similar to boardinghouses, usually established in crowded neighborhoods of industrial cities. There, settlement workers, who were educated, middle-class men and women, provided services for their poorer neighbors.

The first settlement houses started in London, England, in the 1880s. Hull House was Chicago's first settlement house and the most influential one in the United States.

HISTORY OF HULL HOUSE

In 1888, while on a tour of Europe, Jane Addams and Ellen Gates Starr visited Toynbee Hall, a settlement house in East London. There, students from Oxford University and Cambridge University could, during their vacations, work and live among the poor, helping to improve their lives. When Addams and Starr returned to Chicago, they decided to start a similar project there. In January 1889, Addams and Starr searched for a location for a settlement house. They found a large, abandoned mansion in Chicago that had once been the home of real-estate industrialist Charles Hull. His niece, Helen Culver, agreed to lease it to Addams and Starr. The women moved in on September 18, 1889.

Jane Addams believed that settlement houses were an important contribution to the Progressive movement of social and political **reform** in the United States that had begun in the late 1800s. Addams felt that as long as the upper and lower classes lived separately and had nothing in common, there was nothing holding the country together. They would not support one another's causes because they would always view each other as adversaries. Settlement houses could bring people together, educating both upper- and lower-class participants about the things they had in common. As Addams later wrote in her book *Twenty Years at Hull House*, "I gradually became convinced that it would be a good thing to rent a house in a part of the city where many primitive and actual needs are found, in which young women . . . might restore a balance of activity along traditional lines and learn of life from life itself."

The Hull House neighborhood had once been wealthy, but by the 1880s, it had become a crowded urban neighborhood populated by Italian, Irish, German, Greek, Bohemian, and Russian and Polish Jewish

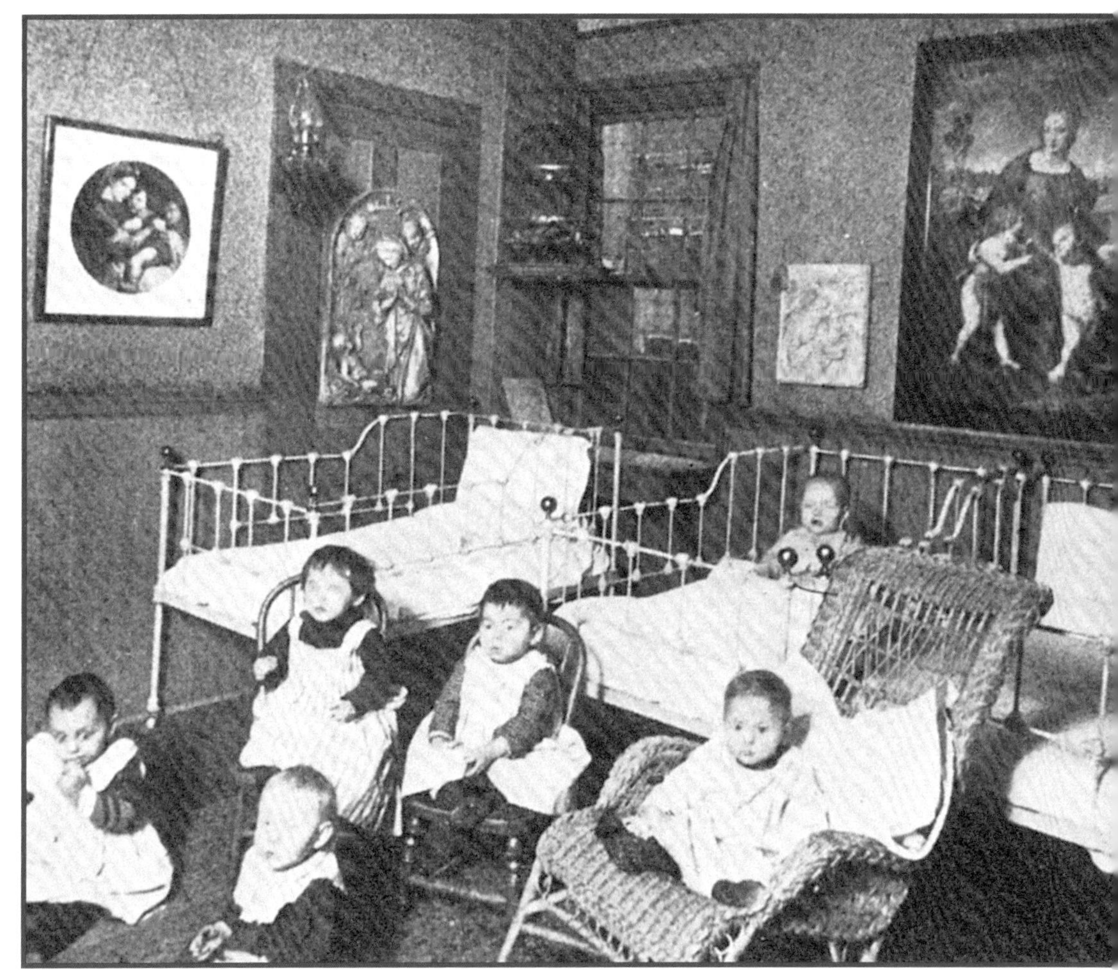

A nursery in Jane Addams's Hull House provided care for the young children of working mothers living on Chicago's west side. Unable to afford appropriate childcare, poor and often desperate women sometimes left their children and babies unattended during the day so they could eke out a living by working in the factories.

immigrants. At first, Addams and Starr invited people in the neighborhood to readings and slide shows, but they soon realized that the women most needed a place to bring their young children. Addams and Starr started a kindergarten at Hull House, and within 3 weeks, they had enrolled 24 children, with many more on the waiting list.

ACTIVITIES AT HULL HOUSE

Hull House strove to introduce its visitors to high culture. It added an art gallery and music school to its offerings. Addams believed that people should be educated about the cultures of other immigrants. She established the Hull House Labor Museum to highlight the lives immigrants led in their country of origin. Addams also set up adult education classes at night and ran a coffeehouse to give visitors a place to relax and meet one another.

Jane Addams later pointed out that the object of the settlement program was to "help the foreign-born conserve and keep whatever of value their past life contained and to bring them into contact with a better class of Americans." A popular part of the program included local residents sharing songs, dances, games, and food from their home country.

Various teachers and social reformers in Chicago were also brought to Hull House to provide free lectures on a variety of topics. This included such esteemed people as women's rights activist Susan B. Anthony, Progressive journalist Ray Stannard Baker, and renowned architect Frank Lloyd Wright.

In 1891, Florence Kelley, a member of the Socialist Labor Party, became a resident at Hull House. She was an experienced political activist, and through her influence, Hull House became a center of social reform. Her presence also attracted other social reformers to the settlement, which led to important reforms and the passage of progressive laws on the local, state, and national levels.

Hull House's residents established Chicago's first public playground and bathhouse and campaigned to reform city politics. They also investigated housing and employment issues and fought for improved public schools.

At the state level, Hull House residents lobbied for protective legislation for women and children, child labor laws, compulsory education, and the protection of immigrants. The bonds formed at Hull House helped create the Juvenile Protection Agency and push child labor laws through the Illinois legislature in 1893. In 1916, the federal government passed similar laws. Additionally, on a national level, Hull House residents and other settlement workers fought for various reforms that were part of the Progressive movement, including national child-labor laws, women's suffrage, and workers' compensation.

EXPANSION OF SETTLEMENT HOUSES

The great success of Hull House led to other settlement houses forming in New York, Boston, Philadelphia, and Chicago. By 1900, there were more than 100 settlement houses in the United States, with 15 in Chicago.

By 1907, the original Hull House had expanded to include 13 buildings that covered nearly an entire city block. The new structures included a gymnasium, theater, art gallery, music school, boys' club, auditorium, cafeteria, kindergarten, nursery, libraries, post office, meeting and club rooms, art studios, kitchen, and a dining room and apartments for the residential staff. The new, expanded Hull House attracted thousands of people each week from the surrounding neighborhood.

Jane Addams remained head resident of Hull House until her death in 1935. Hull House continued to be active until the 1960s, when the

Hull House in the 1890s and 2000s

The mission of Hull House, as Jane Addams noted in 1889, was to, "aid in the solutions of life in a great city, to help our neighbors build responsible, self-sufficient lives for themselves and their families." The settlement house was a means for serving the poor in urban areas by living among them and serving them directly. As the settlement house staffs learned efficient ways of helping immigrants and the city's poor, they worked to transfer long-term responsibility for their social programs to government agencies. Settlement house workers also pioneered the profession of modern social work.

Although cofounder Jane Addams died in 1935, Hull House continued its work on the city's Near West Side until the 1960s. At that time, the area around Hull House was set aside for the campus of the new University of Illinois (now UIC). The original Hull House mansion was turned into a museum. Today, Hull House still operates a community center and continues to provide programs for those in need across Chicago.

In 2009, the National Endowment for the Humanities gave the University of Illinois at Chicago a $350,000 grant to expand some of the permanent exhibits at the Hull House Museum. The grant also will support a new exhibit, "Jane Addams and the Hull House Settlement: Redefining Democracy." This exhibit will nearly double the exhibition space in the Hull House mansion. Some of the money also will be used to recreate Addams's second-floor bedroom, an area previously closed to the public. Plans include displaying many of Addams's personal artifacts, including her childhood rocking chair, the desk where she wrote, letters, and telegrams.

buildings were displaced by the new college campus of the University of Illinois. The original Hull House building is now a museum, part of the College of Architecture and the Arts at the university and a reminder of an era of change.

See also: Addams, Jane; Child Labor.

Further Reading

Addams, Jane. *Twenty Years at Hull House.* New York: New American Library Classics, 1999.

Glowacki, Peggy, and Julia Hendry. *Hull House.* Mount Pleasant, S.C.: Arcadia Publishers, 2004.

Interstate Commerce Act (1887)

Passed by the U.S. Congress in 1887, bill that established federal regulation of the railroad industry. One of many progressive reforms passed during the late 1800s and early 1900s, the Interstate Commerce Act made railroads the first American industry to be regulated by the federal government.

The act required that railroads charge their customers fair rates that would be made public. The act also created the Interstate Commerce Commission (ICC), a federal agency that could investigate and sue companies that did not follow the law. The ICC was given widespread power, and it would later become the model of other regulatory agencies for private businesses in the United States. The act, in part, noted:

> That the Commission hereby created shall have authority to inquire into the management of the business of all common carriers subject to the provisions of this act, and shall keep itself informed as to the manner and method in which the same is conducted, and shall have the right to obtain from such common carriers full and complete information necessary to enable the Commission to perform the duties and carry out the objects for which it was created; and for the purposes of this act the Commission shall have power to require the attendance and testimony of witnesses and the production of all books, papers, tariffs, contracts, agreements, and documents relating to any matter under investigation, and to that end may invoke the aid of any court of the United States in requiring the attendance and testimony of witnesses and the production of books, papers, and documents under the provisions of this section.

THE GROWTH OF MONOPOLIES

With the growth of business during the second half of the 1800s, many Americans became concerned about the increasing power and wealth of corporations. Many large corporations had become **monopolies**, or companies that control an entire industry. When a company becomes a monopoly, it can set high prices for its goods because it has little or no competition. Progressives, who sought reform in nearly every part of American society at the time, argued that the federal government needed to regulate big businesses in order to prevent monopolies.

Many railroad companies had easily become monopolies during the late 1800s because often only one railroad company serviced an entire area. Without competition, the railroad company could charge very high fares to its customers, who would be forced to pay them. Some railroad companies also formed trusts, agreements made by groups of companies to fix or hold prices, thereby ending competition. This meant that many railroad companies agreed on charging equally high rates to their customers.

Because the railroad industry was unregulated, there were many other abusive practices. Sometimes, railroads gave **rebates**, or discounts, to large businesses to ensure that the businesses would only use that railroad company. This prevented other railroads from serving those businesses. Larger railroad companies sometimes lowered prices so much that they forced smaller companies out of business. Then they would raise their prices. Railroads often charged more for short hauls than for long hauls, a scheme that effectively discriminated against smaller businesses. These schemes resulted in bankruptcy for many rail carriers and their customers.

DEMAND FOR REFORM
By the 1880s, many Americans had become concerned by the abuses within the railroad industry and demanded reform. Some states had passed their own reform laws for the railroad industry. However, in an 1886 court case, *Wabash, St. Louis, & Pacific Railway Co. v. Illinois*, the U.S. Supreme Court ruled that state laws regulating railroads were unconstitutional because they violated the Commerce Clause, which gives Congress the power "to regulate Commerce with foreign nations, and among the several States, and with the Indian Tribes."

This did not stop Americans from demanding reform within the railroad industry; in the following year, 1887, Congress responded by passing the Interstate Commerce Act, which President Grover Cleveland (1885–1889, 1893–1897) signed into law. The law had been supported by both major political parties, Republicans and Democrats, from all regions of the country.

First Attempt at Reform The Interstate Commerce Act addressed the problem of railroad monopolies by setting guidelines for how the railroads could do business. The act required that railroad rates had to be "reasonable and just," though it did not give the federal government the power to set the rates. It prohibited trusts, rebates, and discriminatory fares. It also required railroad companies to publish their fares and allowed them to change fares only after giving the public 10 days' notice. Finally, it established the Interstate Commerce Commission, which could investigate and sue companies who did not follow the law.

The Interstate Commerce Act was the first law to give Congress the right to regulate private companies engaged in interstate commerce. However, the law in practice was not always easy to enforce. There were no clear definitions of what made something a "discriminatory practice." The most effective part of the Interstate Commerce Act was its requirement that railroads submit annual reports to the Interstate Commerce Committee.

Limited Power The power of the Interstate Commerce Commission was limited. The organization was only authorized to investigate companies whose business crossed over state lines. If the railroad only operated within one state, the Interstate Commerce Commission did not have any authority over it. In general, even if the commission brought a particular railroad company to court, the courts usually ruled in favor of the company. Still, the greatest significance of the Interstate Commerce Act was that it led to more federal regulation of industry within the United States.

See also: Sherman Antitrust Act (1890).

Johnson, Hiram (1866–1945)

Progressive Republican and governor of California who was known as a great reformer. Johnson was one of the founders of the Progressive Party.

Hiram Johnson was born on September 2, 1866. His father was a Republican member of the House of Representatives and a member of the California state legislature. His mother, a member of the Daughters of the American Revolution, took great pride in her family's patriotic legacy.

EARLY LIFE

Young Johnson was an able though unremarkable student. He got his first job as stenographer, writing notes in shorthand for a law firm. The job gave him an interest in law, and in 1883, he was accepted to the University of California at Berkley, where he earned a law degree. In 1888, he passed the California bar exam and began to practice law in Sacramento, the state capital.

While Hiram had assisted his father in his 1894 campaign for a seat in the House, he broke from his father politically by the time of the next election. Johnson had become more progressive and forward-thinking.

CAREER

In 1902, Johnson moved to San Francisco and took a job as assistant district attorney. He became more politically motivated and began working to end corruption in government. Many members of California's legislature were on the Southern Pacific Railroad payroll, making it difficult to pass any laws that put voter interests ahead of business. To this end, Johnson assisted special federal prosecutor Francis Heney in bringing down corrupt officials in 1908. Mayor Eugene Schmitz and his assistant, Abe Reuf, were arrested for bribery. During the tense trial, however, Heney was shot, and Johnson took over the case. The case was won, in no small measure because of public support and sympathy for Heney, who survived despite being wounded in the head.

Governor In 1910, Johnson was elected governor of California. He was a member of the Lincoln-Roosevelt League, a liberal Republican organization founded to combat corruption in California. The league succeeded in requiring political parties to select candidates by **primary elections**, in which voters select the parties' nominees. Hiram Johnson was the first candidate elected under the primary system.

As governor, Johnson pushed through a number of **reforms**. One of the most influential was changing the way senators were elected. Originally, as required by the U.S. Constitution, the California state legislature had chosen senators. Johnson passed a law that changed the system to an election in which voters cast ballots recommending their choices to the legislature. The state legislature was then to follow the voters' selection.

His populist ideas also included policies meant to empower individual citizens. Among these were the introduction in 1911 of **initiative**, **referendum**, and **recall** powers to the people. These powers allow citizens to put motions on the ballot for direct election, as opposed to waiting for members of the legislature to propose a law, enabling a more direct form of democracy. However, California is the only state with such initiative and referendum laws. These powers remain hotly debated today, because laws may be passed that require government expenditures without simultaneously passing a way to fund them.

In 1912, Johnson and other progressive California Republicans attended the Republican National Convention in Chicago. The more progressive Republicans were outnumbered. When the convention selected Taft as their presidential nominee, Johnson, former president Theodore Roosevelt (1901–1909), and other Progressives left to form the Progressive Party. Roosevelt ran as the presidential nominee, while Johnson ran as his vice president. Both the Republicans and Progressives lost the election to Democrat Woodrow Wilson (1913–1921).

Senator Johnson went on to a career in the U.S. Senate that lasted until his death in 1945. He was very popular in his home state of California, winning 94.5 percent of the popular vote in his 1934 reelection bid. He supported Franklin Delano Roosevelt's (1933–1945) **New Deal** policies, although he disagreed with Roosevelt on foreign policy. Johnson was always a strict **isolationist** and therefore opposed U.S. participation in the League of Nations and the United Nations (UN). In fact, he is the only U.S. senator to have voted against the nation's entry into both international organizations.

Johnson died on August 6, 1945. He continues to be remembered as one of the greatest reformers in California history. In 2009, California's governor and first lady, Arnold Schwarzenegger and Maria Shriver, announced that Johnson would be one of 13 inductees into the California Hall of Fame that year.

See also: Election of 1912.

Further Reading

Lower, Richard. *A Bloc of One: The Political Career of Hiram W. Johnson*. Stanford, Calif.: Stanford University Press, 1993.

H–L

La Follette, Robert (1855–1925)

Greatly influential politician of the early twentieth century; a leader who brought **progressive** reforms to his home state of Wisconsin and worked to implement those changes nationally. Robert La Follette was a radical progressive Republican who became governor of Wisconsin and a member of the U.S. Senate.

EARLY LIFE

Born in Primrose, Wisconsin, on June 14, 1885, La Follette had a rural upbringing. His father died when he was eight months old, and his mother remarried when he was six. His stepfather encouraged him to study law.

In 1875, La Follette was accepted to the University of Wisconsin. He was a poor student but led an active social life. He excelled at public speaking and used his oratory skills to entertain his classmates. He entered speaking competitions and eventually won the Inter-State Oratorical Contest. His skills were even praised in the local Madison newspaper. Still, despite his abilities as a speaker, he only narrowly graduated from college.

In 1882, La Follette married a former classmate, Belle Case. She was an excellent student and highly praised by her professors for her sharp mind. She and Robert were both independent, radical thinkers. Belle became the first woman to get a law degree from the University of Wisconsin Law School, and she was able to balance her home life with a life of public speaking.

Armed with his own law degree obtained in 1880, La Follette started a campaign to become district attorney of Dane County. He was well liked by the community, respected as a lawyer, and easily won the election. He served two terms as district attorney and then ran for a seat in the U.S. House of Representatives.

In 1884, La Follette was elected to the House, where he served for three terms. His efforts were focused on reining in the government and advocating for Native American and African American rights. La Follette was already gaining a reputation for defending unpopular positions, even from those in his own party. He would not vote for anything he did not actually support, and he would not be coerced. La Follette always advocated for citizens, putting himself in opposition to big business and government corruption. In 1890, La Follette lost his seat in the House, a victim of a nationwide movement to sweep the Republicans from office.

COMMITTED REFORMER

Back home in Wisconsin, La Follette's progressive sentiments began to truly take root. When he was offered a bribe to influence the outcome of a case his brother was presiding over, it became clear to him that that politics needed to be overhauled. In addition to corruption, he felt that his own political party was in the pocket of the railroads, which meant that business interests were taking precedent over those of citizens. Determined to change this, at least in his own state, La Follette began gathering a group of political supporters to help him battle the **political machine** of his own party to gain the nomination for governor. In 1900, he had earned enough personal influence to win the nomination and the election.

CALL FOR PRIMARY ELECTIONS

One of the first major progressive reforms for which La Follette fought was a switch to the **primary election** system for selecting candidates. The Republican Party had been using a caucus system, in which party members selected candidates, without input from the public. Primaries would allow citizens to vote, giving them more control over the government. La Follette was a passionate speaker, and even his adversaries respected his efforts. His speeches drew large crowds, and he would sometimes give more than one speech a day as he campaigned.

La Follette won the nomination for governor again in 1904. In addition to campaigning for himself, he campaigned for a more progressive

Republican ticket in general. During his speeches, he would read out the voting records of Republicans in office, hoping that the embarrassing records would speak for themselves. The tactic worked, and in 1904, progressive Republicans gained a majority in the state legislature.

THE NATION'S LEGISLATIVE LEADER

With the power to get their legislation through at last, La Follette and his Progressives passed laws to limit the influence of the railroads. They also passed laws to limit lobbying. Under La Follette's leadership, the state government began working in concert with the University of Wisconsin in writing legislation. Called the Wisconsin Idea, it was a philosophy that stated that universities should use their research capacities to develop solutions to social, political, and health problems. Progressive causes, such as **worker's compensation** for injuries gained on the job, and progressive taxation were among the ideas to come from the collaboration of universities and government.

Having established an era of Progressivism in Wisconsin, La Follette moved on to the U.S. Senate in 1906, where he championed many of the same causes to great acclaim. He attempted to run for president in 1924 under the banner of his own Progressive Party. The 1924 party platform called for widespread reforms in the nation. Among them were:

1. We pledge a complete housecleaning in the Department of Justice, the Department of the Interior, and the other executive departments. We demand that the power of the Federal Government be used to crush private monopoly, not to foster it.
2. We pledge recovery of the navy's oil reserves and all other parts of the public domain which have been fraudulently or illegally leased. . . . We favor public ownership of the nation's water power and the creation and development of a national super-water-power system. . . .
3. . . . We declare for public ownership of railroads with definite safeguards against bureaucratic control, as the only final solution of the transportation problem.
4. We favor reduction of Federal taxes upon individual incomes and legitimate business. . . .
5. . . . We favor [an] amendment to the constitution . . . to provide for the election of all Federal Judges, without party designation, for fixed terms not exceeding ten years, by direct vote of the people.
6. . . . We advocate the calling of a special session of Congress to pass legislation for the relief of American agriculture. . . .
7. . . . We favor prompt ratification of the Child Labor amendment, and subsequent enactment of a Federal law to protect children in industry.

The massive reforms proposed by the Progressive Party were viewed as too extreme by most Americans. In the election of 1924, La Follette won only the 13 **electoral votes** of his home state of Wisconsin. Nationwide, however, he received 17 percent of the vote, the third highest percentage for any **third-party candidate** since the formation of the modern two-party system following the Civil War (1861–1865).

After La Follete's defeat, the Progressive Party disbanded. La Follette, who continued to serve in the U.S. Senate as a Republican until his death, died on June 20, 1925, in Washington, D.C. His children and grandchildren carried on his legacy of progressive politics into the 1980s.

See also: Child Labor; Progressive Party.

Further Reading

Unger, Nancy C. *Fighting Bob La Follette: The Righteous Reformer.* Chapel Hill: University of North Carolina Press, 2000.

M–N

McClure's Magazine *(1893–1929)*

A literary and political magazine founded by journalist Samuel McClure in 1893. *McClure's Magazine* is considered to be the first American magazine to feature **muckraking** journalism, or investigative reports written by **progressive** journalists who exposed corruption in American society.

McClure's initially published stories of popular writers of the day, including the English novelist Rudyard Kipling, the American novelist Jack London, and the British detective story writer Arthur Conan Doyle. The magazine cost only 15 cents, making it cheaper than other literary magazines of its time. By 1902, however, *McClure's* began to specialize in muckraking journalism, expressing the views of Samuel McClure and his staff. McClure supported many of the **reforms** associated with the Progressive movement of the late 1800s and early 1900s, including government **regulation** of business and reforms in taxes and the election process. He encouraged his reporters to search out the truth and to expose **corruption** in American society.

THE FIRST MUCKRAKERS

Progressive journalist Ida Tarbell (1857–1944) wrote the first muckraking article for *McClure's* in 1902. Previously, Tarbell had made her name as a journalist with popular articles for *McClure's* about French leader Napoleon Bonaparte (r. 1804–1814, 1815) and Abraham Lincoln (1861–1865).

In 1900, Tarbell began to research John D. Rockefeller's Standard Oil Company. Tarbell had grown up in the oil regions of western Pennsylvania, and the topic was of interest to her. Tarbell's interviews with Standard Oil partner Henry Rogers revealed how Rockefeller's business practices had destroyed smaller oil businesses in Pennsylvania. Tarbell pointed out that Standard Oil "had never played fair, and that ruined their greatness for me." Her work first ran as a series of articles in *McClure's*; the articles were published together in 1904 as a book, *The History of the Standard Oil Company*. In her book, Tarbell described how the independent oil producers ultimately lost the fight with Standard Oil:

The August 1905 cover of *McClure's Magazine* shows a young woman relaxing, taking a break from her reading. *McClure's* attractive covers and low price helped ensure a wide readership among the nation's middle class.

> The great human tragedies of the Oil Regions lie in the individual compromises which followed the public settlement of 1880. For then it was that man after man, from hopelessness, from disgust, from ambition, from love of money, gave up the fight for principle which he had waged for seven years. . . . This man took a position with the Standard and became henceforth active in its business; that man took a salary and dropped out of sight; this one went his independent way, but with closed lips; that one shook the dust of the Oil Regions from his feet and went out to seek "God's Country," asking only that he should never again hear the word "oil." The newspapers bowed to the victor. A sudden hush came over the region, the hush of defeat, of cowardice, of hopelessness.

The popularity of Tarbell's articles encouraged another progressive journalist, Lincoln Steffens, to follow another scandal. Steffens set out to expose corruption in city government, starting with St. Louis, Missouri. After publishing his article, Samuel McClure sent Steffens to investigate corruption in the city government of Minneapolis, Minnesota. Steffens's reports were eventually published as a series of collected articles in 1904 called *Shame of the Cities*. Like Ida Tarbell, Steffens wanted to bring about reform and hoped that Americans would become outraged by these stories of bribes and other unfair practices in city politics and push for change.

Another progressive journalist, Ray Stannard Baker, was sent by Samuel McClure to the coalfields of Wilkes-Barre, Pennsylvania, to report on a months-long strike by the United Mine Workers (UMW). McClure was most interested in the nonunion miners, who had continued to work despite the strike. Baker's article, "The Right to Work," exposed abuses of union leaders and sympathetically described the hardships of the nonstriking miners.

The public response to these investigative reports was huge. The sharp **exposés** written by Ida Tarbell, Lincoln Steffens, Ray Stannard Baker, and others instantly boosted *McClure's* readership and made it the leading magazine for progressive journalism. Other popular magazines of the time, including *Everybody's, Pearson's, Cosmopolitan*, and *Collier's*, soon picked up on the trend. By 1904, all had began to publish articles that exposed political, legal, and financial corruption in American society.

THE DECLINE OF MCCLURE'S

President Theodore Roosevelt (1901–1909) was initially a big supporter of the kind of progressive journalism found in *McClure's*. He, too, believed that exposing corruption would help lead to the passage of new laws to reform American society.

However, when journalist David Graham Phillips published an article in *Cosmopolitan* entitled "The Treason in the Senate," attacking some of Roosevelt's political allies, Roosevelt responded with a speech in April 1906 in which he denounced investigative journalists as "muckrakers." Roosevelt compared them to a character in John Bunyan's novel *Pilgrim's Progress* (1678)—a character described as "the man who could look no way but downward with the muckrake in his hands." Roosevelt claimed that many journalists were turning away from reporting on positive accounts of American life in favor of "raking up the muck." Soon after Roosevelt's speech, public demand for muckraking journalism declined. Even many Progressives had grown tired of these journalistic crusades for truth and justice.

At the same time, just a few months after Roosevelt's speech, most of the writing staff of *McClure's* left because of clashes with Samuel McClure over business practices; they formed *The American Magazine*. McClure continued to publish his magazine, with future acclaimed American novelist Willa Cather as managing editor, until debt forced him to sell it to creditors in 1911. *McClure's Magazine* was eventually redesigned as a women's magazine, but sales declined in the late 1920s. The last issue appeared in March 1929.

See also: Muckrakers; Roosevelt, Theodore; Social Justice; Steffens, Lincoln; Tarbell, Ida.

McKinley, William (1843–1901)

Twenty-fifth president of the United States. William McKinley's election in 1896 began the Progressive Era, a period of widespread social and political **reform** that lasted until the early 1900s.

EARLY LIFE

McKinley was born on January 28, 1843, in Niles, Ohio, to William and Nancy McKinley. He was the seventh of nine children. In 1852, the family moved to Poland, Ohio, where William attended the Poland Academy, a prestigious school of advanced learning. He graduated in 1859 and went on to Allegheny College for one year. Like many young men of the time, when the Civil War broke out in 1861 McKinley enlisted in the army. He was 18 years old.

McKinley served in an Ohio **regiment** under future president Rutherford B. Hayes (1877–1881). He proved to be a brave and accomplished soldier, earning himself a promotion due to his actions at the Battle of Antietam, the bloodiest single battle of the Civil War (1861–1865). McKinley was discharged in 1865 and returned home to Ohio.

Back in Ohio, McKinley began studying law under the guidance of Judge Charles Glidden. The next year, 1866, he began his formal education at Albany Law School in New York, although he did not graduate from this school either. Regardless, he passed the bar in 1867 and began practicing law. He also began involving himself in politics and joined the Republican Party, working on behalf of his former commander, Rutherford B. Hayes.

CAREER

In 1877, McKinley was elected to the House of Representatives. He served there until 1891. During his tenure, he was chairman of the Committee of Ways and Means, responsible for legislation on taxes and tariffs. McKinley supported protective tariffs and wrote the McKinley Tariff of 1890. The tariff was widely unpopular, as it raised the taxes on imported goods to the highest level in history up to that point. Farmers were particularly hard hit; goods now cost them more, but their products were unprotected and suffered low rates on the world market. The McKinley Tariff was instrumental in the Democratic takeover of the government in the 1890 election.

McKinley lost reelection but did not bow out of politics. In the 1892 election, he ran for and won the governorship of Ohio. It was a first step on the path toward the presidency. In 1896, he won his party's nomination and ran against William Jennings Bryan, a **Populist** and Democratic politician who supported many important reforms. The central issue of their debates was the country's financial system. McKinley wanted the United States to retain the gold standard for backing its currency, while Bryan wanted a gold and silver standard.

McKinley won the election handily. As he had as a congressman, McKinley supported protective tariffs and passed the Dingley Act, which again raised import duties to the highest level yet seen. McKinley also got the country involved in the Spanish-American War (1898), which resulted in the appropriation of the new territories of Guam, Puerto Rico, and the Philippines.

Although he had always supported protectionist policies, when he was reelected in 1900 McKinley began to see the advantages of encouraging foreign trade. He was never able to implement these plans. On September 6, 1901, at the Pan American Exposition in Buffalo, New York, McKinley was shot by **anarchist** Leon Frank Czolgosz. Czolgosz did not believe in government or rulers and came to the Buffalo Exposition with the sole purpose of assassinating President McKinley. Though doctors tried to treat McKinley, he died from his wounds a week later. Vice President Theodore Roosevelt was sworn in as president and a new era of **progressive** reform began.

See also: Roosevelt, Theodore.

Further Reading

Phillips, Kevin. *William McKinley*. New York: Times Books, 2003.

Muckrakers

Investigative reporters, novelists, and critics who exposed acts of **corruption** and unfairness in American politics and business during the early 1900s. President Theodore Roosevelt (1901–1909) is credited with using the term *muckrakers*. During a speech in 1906, Roosevelt compared investigative journalists to a character in John Bunyan's novel *Pilgrim's Progress* (1678) who was described as "the man who could look no way but downward with the muck-rake in his hands; who would neither look up nor regard the crown he was offered, but continued to rake to himself the filth on the floor." Roosevelt called these writers "muckrakers" because he felt that their main concern was only to "rake up muck," or to seek scandal and portray the worst evils in society. The term stuck.

MUCKRAKING JOURNALISM

McClure's Magazine, founded in 1893, is considered to be the first American magazine to feature muckraking journalism. In 1902, **progressive** journalist Ida Tarbell wrote a series of articles for *McClure's*, exposing the **unethical** business practices of John D. Rockefeller's Standard Oil Company. Reporter Lincoln Steffens followed with a series of articles exposing corruption in city government; these were later published in a collection called *Shame of the Cities*. Other popular magazines of the time, including *Everybody's*, *Pearson's*, *Cosmopolitan*, and *Collier's*, soon picked up on the trend and began to publish muckraking articles that exposed political, legal, and financial corruption in American society.

Jacob Riis became famous as a muckraker after the publication of his book *How the Other Half Lives* (1890), which depicted the miserable living conditions of **immigrants** in city **tenement** buildings. However, perhaps the most famous muckraking book of the era was Upton Sinclair's 1906 novel, *The Jungle*, which exposed the terrible working conditions and extremely unsanitary practices of the meatpacking plants in Chicago.

THEODORE ROOSEVELT AND THE MUCKRAKERS

President Theodore Roosevelt was very responsive to investigative journalism. Like the muckrakers, Roosevelt believed that exposing corruption would help lead to the passage of new laws to reform American society. For example, after the publication of *The Jungle*, Roosevelt persuaded Congress to pass the Pure Food and Drug Act and the Meat Inspection Act, both in 1906. However, when journalist David Graham Phillips published an article in *Cosmopolitan* that same year entitled "The Treason in the Senate," attacking some of Roosevelt's political allies, Roosevelt responded with the speech that denounced these journalists as muckrakers.

Most investigative journalists did not like being described as muckrakers. They felt betrayed by President Roosevelt, a man who had once supported their efforts. Years later, Ida Tarbell defended muckraking: "There is a great difference between a sensational presentation of a public scandal for the sake of making a good story, and a serious study of situations which are making the public uneasy." Yet soon after Roosevelt's speech, public demand for muckraking journalism declined. Even many Progressives had grown tired of these journalistic crusades for truth and justice. Today, however, muckrakers are still acknowledged for the important work they did and the various governmental reforms that resulted from their investigations.

See also: McClure's Magazine; Riis, Jacob; Roosevelt, Theodore; Sinclair, Upton; Social Justice; Steffens, Lincoln; Tarbell, Ida.

Further Reading

Bausum, Ann. *Muckrakers: How Ida Tarbell, Upton Sinclair, and Lincoln Steffens Helped Expose Scandal, Inspire Reform, and Invent Investigative Journalism*. Des Moines, Iowa: National Geographic Children's Books, 2007.

Nineteenth Amendment (1920)

Amendment to the U.S. Constitution that gave women the right to vote in all federal, state, and local elections. The women's **suffrage** movement was born in 1848 at the Woman's Rights Convention held in Seneca Falls, New York. Suffragists encouraged women to assert their right to vote after the passage of the Fourteenth Amendment in 1868, which granted citizenship to and protected the civil rights of recently freed slaves.

Suffragists claimed that under the equal protection clause of the Fourteenth Amendment, women were also granted the right to vote. Their attempts to test this right failed. Suffragist Susan B. Anthony was arrested and convicted for trying to vote in the 1872 presidential election in Rochester, New York.

The suffrage movement had some success in the western states. As a territory, Wyoming extended full suffrage to women in 1869 and retained it upon becoming a state in 1890. Colorado, Utah, and Idaho also granted women voting rights before the turn of the century. After that, however, suffragists encountered stronger opposition. It was not until the height of the **Progressive** Era that other states, mostly in the West, gave women full voting rights.

A woman enters a voting booth in 1920 to cast her first ballot. After the ratification of the Nineteenth Amendment, women throughout the United States were eligible to vote.

Washington granted equal suffrage in 1910; California in 1911; Arizona, Kansas, and Oregon in 1912; Montana and Nevada in 1914; and New York in 1917.

CONSTITUTIONAL AMENDMENT

On the eve of World War I (1914–1918), those who favored militant tactics took the lead in a national campaign for women's rights. President Woodrow Wilson's (1913–1921) opposition to a constitutional amendment caused a series of demonstrations by suffragists around the White House after the United States had entered the war. The protesters insisted that it was wrong for this country to deny its own female citizens a right to participate in government while at the same time it was fighting a war to make "the world safe for **democracy.**"

Finally, President Wilson changed his mind, announcing on January 9, 1918, his support for the proposed suffrage amendment. The House of Representatives approved it the next day by a 274-136 vote, one vote more than the necessary two-thirds majority. The Senate, however, fell short of the two-thirds majority in October 1918 and again in February 1919. Nevertheless, when the Congress elected in November 1918 met for the first time on May 19, 1919, it took little more than two weeks to gain the required majorities in both chambers.

APPROVAL

On August 18, 1920, Tennessee became the 36th state to have the

Suffrage for Women

The Nineteenth Amendment extended suffrage to women. The amendment was the result of the work of many social reformers and other activists, going back to at least 1848. The proposed amendment was introduced into Congress every year beginning in 1872, without success. To raise awareness of the issue, one suffragist group, the Silent Sentinels, protested in front of the White House for 18 long months, starting in 1917.

On January 9, 1918, President Woodrow Wilson announced his support of the amendment. The next day, the House of Representatives narrowly passed the amendment, but the Senate refused to even debate it until October. When the Senate voted on the amendment in October, it still failed by three votes. Finally, on May 21, 1919, the House of Representatives passed the amendment by a vote of 304 to 89, and the Senate followed suit on June 4—by a vote of 56 to 25. The states ratified the amendment quickly, and it was officially added to the Constitution on August 26, 1920. Thus, women across the nation were able to vote in the presidential election of 1920. The amendment consists of two brief sections:

> Section 1. The right of citizens of the United States to vote shall not be denied or abridged by the United States or by any state on account of sex.
>
> Section 2. Congress shall have power to enforce this article by appropriate legislation.

amendment **ratified**, enough for approval. On August 26, Secretary of State Bainbridge Colby signed a proclamation formally adding the Nineteenth Amendment to the U.S. Constitution.

See also: Anthony, Susan B; Stanton, Elizabeth Cady; Suffragists.

FURTHER READING

Clift, Eleanor. *Founding Sisters and the Nineteenth Amendment*. New York: Wiley, 2003.

Koutras Bozonelis, Helen. *A Look at the Nineteenth Amendment: Women Win the Right to Vote.* Berkeley Heights, N.J.: Enslow Publishers, 2008.

Norris, George W. (1861–1944)

Progressive senator from Nebraska responsible for supporting government **reform** and especially the public ownership of hydroelectric plants. Having grown up poor in frontier territory gave George Norris a strong sense of justice and morality. He felt the struggle of the unfortunate was the greatest hurdle for **democracy**—not the protection of the rich.

EARLY LIFE

Norris was born on July 11, 1861, in Sandusky County, Ohio, to Chauncey and Mary Magdalene Norris. They were poor farmers who had moved westward from their home in New York seeking a better life. Both of George's parents were uneducated; although they could read, they could not write.

In 1864, George's father died, leaving George as the only male in the family. Because she was uneducated herself, George's mother instilled in him an appreciation for education. Though the family had little money, she spent what they had and struggled to send all her children to local schools, high school, and finally Baldwin University.

Like his sisters before him, Norris completed one year at Baldwin University and returned home. By age 15, Norris had already adopted the Republican leanings of his neighbors. He was as much raised in the party as he was raised in religion and took great joy in celebrating the 1876 election of fellow Ohioan Rutherford B. Hayes (1877–1881).

Norris next attended university in Valparaiso. He graduated with a degree in law in 1883. In 1885, Norris moved to a farm his mother owned near Tecumseh, Nebraska. This did not last long, and he moved again, to Beaver City, Nebraska.

CAREER

Norris spent the next decade building his law practice and starting his political career. In 1902, he won a seat in the House of Representatives. As a member of the House, he broke with his own party to lead a movement to change the powers of the Speaker of the House. Up until that time, the Speaker could control which bills came to a vote because the Speaker controlled appointments to the Rules Committee, which set the rules for how and when a bill would be debated. In 1910, Norris led a group of representatives in passing a resolution to limit the powers of the Speaker. While his party was not pleased by the break in ranks, Norris established himself as a man who placed ethics above **partisanship**.

In 1912, Norris was elected to the Senate. He spent the rest of his career there. As in the House, Norris followed his conscience rather than the party line.

In 1917, Norris found himself on the losing side of the vote to enter World War I (1914–1918). He believed that the country was being drawn into the war because of the greed of big business. He felt that potential profits were not a good enough reason to join the war. He was attacked in the press, but by explaining himself to the voters, he was able to win reelection.

Norris's most notable contribution to the country was the Twentieth Amendment (1933). This amendment adjusted the dates on which the president, vice president, and newly elected members of

Congress took office, and it eliminated the **lame duck** session of Congress, which was held in every even year. Prior to the **ratification** of this amendment, the president and vice president took office on March 4, and congressional officials took office on March 3. This meant that there were four months following the election in which officials who had been voted out could continue to vote, or fail to vote, on bills. Congress was required to hold a shorter session between the election and March dates, which came to be known as the lame duck session. These "lame ducks" could no longer be held accountable for their actions in Congress, making them unproductive at best and leaving open the opportunity for vindictive behavior.

Norris's action in Congress permanently changed the democratic process in the United States. In 1943, he left Congress and returned home to Nebraska. He died on September 2, 1944.

Further Reading

Norris, George. *Fighting Liberal: The Autobiography of George W. Norris*. Lincoln: University of Nebraska Press, 1992.

Pappas, Christine. *Fighting Statesman: Senator George Norris*. Kansas City, Mo.: Acorn Books, 2001.

P–R

Payne–Aldrich Tariff Act (1909)

Bill passed by the U.S. Congress in 1909 and named for Republican representative Sereno Payne of New York and Republican senator Nelson Aldrich of Rhode Island. The Payne-Aldrich Tariff Act lowered certain **tariffs**, or taxes, on goods entering the United States. It was the first change in American tariff laws since the Dingley Act of 1897.

CONFLICT OVER TARIFFS

Most big American companies favored high tariffs on foreign goods because that forced foreign companies to increase their prices. This meant that American-made goods could be sold at higher prices and still compete with foreign goods. Many Republican leaders who supported big business also favored high tariffs. They argued that these tariffs protected American industry as a whole and therefore benefited all Americans.

Progressives in the Republican Party, however, who often attacked big business, wanted to lower tariff rates so that prices would drop for consumers. They also argued that, instead of tariffs on goods, Americans should pay an income tax based on what they earned, which they believed was fairer. When Republican William Howard Taft (1909–1913) ran for president in the 1908 election, he promised to lower the tariff rates in line with the Progressives.

In 1909, President Taft held a special session in Congress to address the issue of tariffs. Representative Sereno Payne of New York presented a bill that reduced tariffs, and it immediately passed in the House. The bill was then sent to the Senate for passage. However, the Senate instead substituted a bill written by Nelson Aldrich of Rhode Island that called for fewer reductions in some tariffs and increases in others. After progressive Republicans in the Senate attacked the Aldrich bill, a compromise bill was adopted; it added more than 800 amendments to Payne's original. Ultimately, the bill lowered 650 tariffs, raised 220, and left more than 1,000 other tariffs unchanged.

REPUBLICANS DIVIDE ON TARIFF ISSUE

Progressive Republicans demanded that President Taft **veto**, or reject, the bill, since it did not significantly lower tariffs. Instead Taft signed the Payne-Aldrich Tariff Act into law. He also proclaimed it "the best tariff bill that the Republican Party has ever passed. . . ." The bill greatly angered Progressives and further divided the Republican Party.

Former president Theodore Roosevelt (1901–1909) was outraged. When he had endorsed William Howard Taft for president in 1908, he assumed that Taft would carry on Roosevelt's progressive plans for the country. The passage of the Payne-Aldrich Tariff Act proved otherwise. By 1911, Roosevelt had chosen to run against Taft in the upcoming 1912 presidential election. When the Republican Party nominated Taft for reelection, Roosevelt and his followers left the party and formed a new political party. The newly created Progressive Party, nicknamed the "Bull Moose Party," nominated Theodore Roosevelt for president.

The Democratic candidate, New Jersey governor Woodrow Wilson, ultimately won the 1912 election. Roosevelt had taken enough votes away from Taft, splitting the Republican Party and making it impossible for him to win. Taft's support of the Payne-Aldrich Tariff was a major reason he lost the election of 1912.

See also: Bull Moose Party; Election of 1912; Progressive Party; Roosevelt, Theodore; Taft, William Howard.

Progressive Party

An American political party first established in 1912 as an alternative to the two major political parties, the Republican Party and Democratic Party. On three separate occasions, in 1912, 1924, and 1948, the Progressive Party nominated candidates for president of the United States.

ESTABLISHMENT OF THE PARTY

In 1908, President Theodore Roosevelt (1901–1909) encouraged the Republican Party to nominate his close friend, Secretary of War William Howard Taft, to succeed him. When Taft (1909–1913) won the election, Roosevelt assumed that Taft would continue to support his **progressive** plans. However, Taft, who stuck closely to the law and lacked Roosevelt's sharp political skills, proved to be a disappointment to Roosevelt and other Progressives.

REPUBLICAN DISSENT

By 1911, progressive Republicans dissatisfied with President Taft's administration formed the National Progressive Republican League, led by Wisconsin senator Robert La Follette. The group supported Senator La Follette for the Republican presidential nomination in 1912 until former president Theodore Roosevelt decided to run again. Once it became clear that the Republicans would choose Taft as their nominee, Roosevelt endorsed the formation of a new, progressive party. Later that summer, the newly created Progressive Party officially nominated Theodore Roosevelt as its presidential nominee and California senator Hiram Johnson for vice president. Roosevelt claimed he felt "as strong as a bull moose," and soon the Progressive Party was also known as the Bull Moose Party.

Theodore Roosevelt believed that a strong federal government was necessary to regulate industry and protect the working class. His Progressive Party promised various governmental reforms, including the direct popular election of senators, minimum wage standards, prohibition of child labor, and government regulation of business. It also became the first national political party to support women's **suffrage**, or the right to vote. The 1912 Progressive Party platform explained that:

> The conscience of the people, in a time of grave national problems, has called into being a new party, born of the nation's sense of justice. We of the Progressive party here dedicate ourselves to the fulfillment of the duty laid upon us by our fathers to maintain the government of the people, by the people and for the people whose foundations they laid.
>
> We hold with Thomas Jefferson and Abraham Lincoln that the people are the masters of their Constitution, to fulfill its purposes and to safeguard it from those who, by perversion of its intent, would convert it into an instrument of injustice. In accordance with the needs of each generation the people must use their sovereign powers to establish and maintain equal opportunity and industrial justice, to secure which this Government was founded and without which no republic can endure.

Although Roosevelt ultimately lost the presidential election of 1912, he won 27 percent of the popular vote; and he took enough votes away from conservative President Taft to ensure Taft's defeat. The winner of the election was progressive Democrat Woodrow Wilson (1913–1921). The election was still seen as a victory for the Progressives.

THE PROGRESSIVE PARTY REEMERGES

The Progressive Party dropped out of politics not long after the election of 1912, and Roosevelt returned to the Republican Party. In 1924, the Republican Party nominated Calvin Coolidge (1923–1929), a conservative, as its presidential candidate. Coolidge had become president the year before, after the death of President Warren Harding (1921–1923).

Senator Robert La Follette of Wisconsin still strongly believed in progressive reform and was greatly disappointed in Coolidge. In protest, La Follette decided to run for president himself as a candidate of the Progressive Party with Democratic senator Burton K. Wheeler of Montana as his running mate.

Calvin Coolidge easily won the 1924 election. La Follette came in third after Coolidge and the Democratic candidate John W. Davis. Yet because Davis was a conservative Democrat, many liberal Democrats voted for La Follette. As a result, though La Follette won the **electoral votes** of only his home state of Wisconsin, he received almost 5 million votes nationwide.

In 1934, Robert La Follette's son, Robert Jr., who had succeeded his father as Wisconsin senator, left the Republican Party and recreated the Progressive Party at the state level. It soon became Wisconsin's major political party, with Robert La Follette Jr. reelected as the Progressive Party candidate for senator in 1934 and 1938. Philip La Follette, Robert Jr.'s brother, ran for governor of Wisconsin as a Progressive Party candidate and won the elections of 1934 and 1936. The Progressive Party continued in Wisconsin until 1946, when it rejoined the state's Republican Party.

THE PROGRESSIVE PARTY OF 1948

In 1948, a political party called the Progressive Party was created again at the national level by Henry Wallace, though it was unrelated to the party of Theodore Roosevelt and Robert La Follette. Wallace, who had served as vice president under President Franklin D. Roosevelt (1933–1945) from 1941 to 1945, had then become President Harry S. Truman's (1945–1953) secretary of commerce in 1945. Wallace was fired by Truman the following year for publicly opposing Truman's stand against the Soviet Union. In 1948, Wallace decided to run for president as a Progressive Party candidate against Truman, who was running for reelection.

The Progressive Party of 1948 opposed many of Truman's Cold War policies and supported stronger government regulation. However, the Progressive Party's ties to the **Communist Party** damaged its reputation. Therefore, Truman was reelected, and Wallace won only about 2 percent of the vote. Not long after the 1948 election, the Progressive Party crumbled, again disappearing from American politics.

See also: Bull Moose Party; Election of 1912; La Follette, Robert; Taft, William Howard; Wilson, Woodrow.

Further Reading

Chace, James. *1912: Wilson, Roosevelt, Taft and Debs—The Election That Changed the Country.* New York: Simon & Schuster, 2005.

Prohibition

The banning of the sale, manufacture, and transportation of alcohol for consumption in the United States. Prohibition grew out of the **Progressive** movement in the late nineteenth and early twentieth century. Its leaders sought to reform various social and political aspects of American society.

One of the leading **reform** movements during the Progressive Era was the temperance movement, an organized effort to encourage people to moderate or completely stop consuming alcoholic beverages. Many leaders in the temperance movement were women. Those women who had firsthand experiences of the negative effects of liquor on families were strong supporters of a complete ban on alcohol. The temperance movement also appealed to many women because it allowed them a political voice at a time when they could not vote in national elections. The Women's Christian Temperance Union (WCTU), founded in 1874, was at the time the largest women's organization in the country.

THE BREWING INDUSTRY

During this period, the brewing industry had become the most profitable alcohol-refining industry in the country. German immigrants had brought beer to the United States in the early 1800s, and the drink had become popular with many Americans. Beer and whiskey were sold in saloons, businesses that expanded across the country in the late 1800s. In addition to selling alcohol, saloons were often sites of gambling, prostitution, and other illegal activities. For this reason, they were popular targets of prohibitionists, and in 1893, the Anti-Saloon League was formed.

Like the Women's Christian Temperance Union, the Anti-Saloon League focused on implementing antialcohol laws in local communities. As support grew, the league began a campaign to implement Prohibition nationwide. The organization also lobbied members of both political parties, Democrats and Republicans, to support Prohibition. The league sent hundreds of letters and petitions to the U.S. Congress, demanding the prohibition of alcohol.

In 1913, the Anti-Saloon League sponsored a parade in Washington, D.C., in which they presented an amendment to the U.S. Congress. This amendment would be the basis for the Eighteenth Amendment to the U.S. Constitution.

By 1916, 19 states already prohibited the manufacture and sale of alcoholic beverages. Because of increasing pressure from the various organizations of the temperance movement, in December 1917 Congress finally passed the Eighteenth Amendment, which made it illegal to manufacture, distribute, and sell alcoholic beverages. It became law in January 1919, when 36 of the 48 states in the Union had **ratified** it.

PASSAGE OF THE AMENDMENT AND ITS EFFECTS

The wording of the Eighteenth Amendment banned the manufacture and sale of "intoxicating liquors," but many brewers hoped that the ban would not apply to beer and wine. Yet in October 1917, Congress passed the National Prohibition Act, also known as the Volstead Act, named for U.S. representative Andrew Volstead of Minnesota, who sponsored and promoted the bill. The Volstead Act defined intoxicating beverages as anything with more than 0.5 percent

In this hand-tinted photograph from the early 1920s, a federal liquor agent in Chicago destroys illegally made whiskey as a crowd watches. The banning of intoxicating liquors had long been a goal of social reformers, but ultimately, prohibition failed.

alcohol. This meant that beer and wine, as well as whiskey, could not be sold legally. The Volstead Act also established the legal means for the federal government to enforce the Eighteenth Amendment. In January 1920, Prohibition officially went into effect, and all breweries, distilleries, and saloons were forced to shut down.

After the passage of the Eighteenth Amendment, the use of alcoholic beverages was reduced but not eliminated in the United States, as most Prohibition supporters had hoped. Indeed, Prohibition had led to the practice of "bootlegging," or the illegal manufacture, transportation, or sale of alcohol. Some Americans brewed alcohol in their own homes. Some sold their homemade alcohol to secret and illegal bars known as speakeasies, which replaced saloons around the country.

Other bootleggers smuggled alcohol from Canada into the United

States. Many bootleggers became extremely wealthy from their illegal practices and often bribed law enforcement officials, including judges, to avoid prosecution. Bootlegging was profitable because so many people wanted to drink alcohol. Critics of Prohibition argued that it had only led to an increase in illegal activities. It has been estimated that during the late 1920s there were twice as many illegal bars in the United States as there had been legal bars before Prohibition.

Prohibition supporters had not thought that it would be necessary to establish a large administrative agency to enforce the ban on alcohol beverages. The federal government never had more than 2,500 agents enforcing Prohibition, which proved to be too few. By 1925, a number of states had passed laws banning local police from investigating Prohibition violations.

Many Americans who had been part of the temperance movement believed that their work was done once Prohibition went into effect. As a result, many stopped participating in temperance organizations. In addition, a number of antialcohol organizations grew divided as to their role in American society. Some believed that groups like the Anti-Saloon League should focus on enforcing Prohibition by enacting harsher laws. Others argued that educating children about the evils of alcohol was the most important step in prevention. This division weakened the Anti-Saloon League and other organizations at a time when greater support was needed.

PROHIBITION FAILS

By the early 1930s, many Americans had deemed Prohibition a failure. Fiorella LaGuardia, the mayor of New York City from 1934 to 1945, was an outspoken critic of Prohibition. He pointed out that "It is impossible to tell whether prohibition is a good thing or a bad thing. It has never been enforced in this country. There may not be as much liquor in quantity consumed to-day as there was before prohibition, but there is just as much alcohol." In 1932, industrialist John D. Rockefeller, a supporter of Prohibition, noted that "drinking has generally increased, the speakeasy has replaced the saloon; a vast army of lawbreakers has been recruited and financed on a colossal scale."

In addition, Prohibition destroyed the nation's brewing industry. Some companies managed to survive the years of Prohibition by making nonalcoholic beverages, such as root beer and ginger ale, but many went out of business, never to recover. Prohibition also left thousands of people unemployed because of the closings of all the bars, breweries, and distilleries around the country.

During the 1932 election, the Democratic Party made the repeal of Prohibition part of its **platform**. Because the Democrats won both the presidency and a majority in Congress, anti-Prohibition supporters expected swift action.

In February 1933, a resolution proposing a Twenty-first Amendment to repeal the Eighteenth Amendment was introduced into Congress. In December 1933, the Twenty-first Amendment was finally **ratified** by the necessary two-thirds majority of the states. Prohibition had officially ended.

See also: Eighteenth Amendment; Temperance Movement; Twenty-first Amendment.

Further Reading

Lieurance, Suzanne. *The Prohibition Era in American History.* Berkeley Heights, N.J.: Enslow Publishers, 2003.

Lucas, Eileen. *The Eighteenth and Twenty-First Amendments: Alcohol—Prohibition and Repeal.* Berkeley Heights, N.J.: Enslow Publishers, 1998.

Riis, Jacob (1849–1914)

Journalist, photographer, and social reformer. Riis's most famous book, *How the Other Half Lives* (1890), made him a well-known figure of the **Progressive** movement. The book depicted the miserable living conditions of **immigrants** in New York City, bringing their plight to national attention.

Jacob Riis was born to a poor family in Denmark in 1849. He worked as a carpenter until he left for the United States in 1870 in search of a better life. At the time Riis arrived in New York City, many American cities were facing a population explosion. It was especially hard for immigrants to find work or even a place to live. Riis worked for a time as a carpenter but was often unemployed and sometimes had to sleep on the streets.

CAREER AS A REFORMER

Eventually, Riis found work with a news bureau in New York in 1873. Four years later, he became a police reporter for the *New York Tribune*, covering Manhattan's Lower East Side, a poor, mostly immigrant neighborhood. Having had firsthand experience with poverty, Riis was determined to bring the hardships of poor immigrants to light. In 1888, while working for the *New York Evening Sun,* another New York newspaper, Riis began to photograph the slums of New York, including families in their airless, overcrowded apartments. Riis was one of the first photographers to use flash powder, a recent invention. This allowed him to photograph the dimly lit interiors of rear **tenements,** buildings that faced other buildings and had no access to light.

In December 1889, Riis's essays and photographs appeared in *Scribner's Magazine*. The following year, a full-length book, *How the Other Half Lives,* was published. Riis's essays highlighted the miserable conditions his photographs depicted: "One, two, three beds are there, if the old boxes and heaps of foul straw can be called by that name; a broken stove with crazy pipe from which the smoke leaks at every joint, a table of rough boards propped up on boxes, piles of rubbish in the corner. The closeness and smell are appalling. How many people sleep here?"

His book shocked many wealthy New Yorkers, who had no idea what living conditions were like just a few miles away from their own neighborhoods. This was Riis's intention. He believed that citizens would help the poor when they saw for themselves how "the other half" lived. Unlike those who believed that poverty was

One of Jacob Riis's most famous photographs, "Bandit's Roost," taken in 1887, reveals the horrible and dangerous living conditions of New York City's poor. The city's immigrants were not only destitute, but they also faced the possibility of being robbed on a daily basis.

the fault of the victims, Riis and other reformers argued that poverty was the result of environmental conditions and could be changed.

ONGOING SUCCESS

How the Other Half Lives made Jacob Riis famous. It also brought him to the attention of New York police commissioner Theodore Roosevelt. The two men soon became friends, and Riis sometimes took Roosevelt along with him to investigate the living conditions of New York City slums. As a result, Roosevelt pushed for new tenement housing laws after he became the governor of New York.

For the rest of his life, Riis continued to write about the problems of the poor. He also traveled around the country giving lectures that included photographs of tenement life. His popular autobiography, *The Making of an American* (1901), told of his rise from poverty to becoming a social reformer and friend of Theodore Roosevelt (1901–1909), who had become the president of the United States. Jacob Riis died in 1914 at the age of 65.

See also: Muckrakers; Roosevelt, Theodore; Social Justice.

Further Reading

Yochelson, Bonnie, and Daniel Czitrom. *Rediscovering Jacob Riis: The Reformer, His Journalism, and His Photographs.* New York: New Press, 2008.

Roosevelt, Theodore (1858–1919)

A vigorous Republican political leader and the 26th president of the United States. Theodore Roosevelt was a war hero as well as a leader of the 1912 Progressive Party, and was known to be uncompromising in his reforms.

He was born on October 27, 1858, in New York City, to a wealthy family. The Roosevelt family was well established in the upper class of society and owned a number of businesses. While young Roosevelt's father supported the North during the Civil War (1861–1865), his mother was from the South and a Southern sympathizer. In fact, members of his family fought on both sides.

EARLY LIFE

Roosevelt developed an interest in wildlife as a child. The first piece of his zoology collection was the head of a seal that he saw at a market. He used this and other small specimens to learn **taxidermy**. Roosevelt was a small and sickly child. To combat this condition, he began a rigorous exercise regimen and eventually developed a strong, healthy body. Despite advice to the contrary, he adopted "the strenuous life" as the solution to his ailments.

Roosevelt was homeschooled. In 1876, when he was 18, he went to Harvard University in Cambridge, Massachusetts. There, he excelled in the sciences and philosophy. Because of his early interest in animals, he was already considered an accomplished **naturalist**. Roosevelt read avidly, despite poor eyesight, and was noted for having a photographic memory. During his time at Harvard, Roosevelt wrote *The Naval War of 1812*, now considered the first modern historical study of the war. His approach was unbiased. His analysis of the war is still considered an important work.

In 1880, Roosevelt graduated from Harvard. He then attended Columbia Law School in New York but left to run for public office. At age 23, he was elected to the New York House of Representatives. On February 14, 1884, Roosevelt's wife, Alice, and his mother both died. It was a horrendous blow, and Roosevelt refused to speak of Alice again. Later that same year, he attended the Republican National Convention and became disillusioned with his party, as they refused to support the more progressive candidates. Roosevelt did not leave the party, but he did leave politics, retiring to a ranch in South Dakota.

At the ranch, Roosevelt took up hunting with a passion. He lived an active outdoor life and became a deputy sheriff. Roosevelt hunted outlaws and lived a hard frontier life until 1887. A harsh winter killed all the cattle on Roosevelt's ranch, and he returned to his estate at Sagamore Hill, New York.

BACK INTO POLITICS

In 1886, Roosevelt tried to reenter politics by running for mayor of New York. He came in third. That same year, he married Edith Kermit Carow. Roosevelt continued to write and participate in public life. He became president of the American Historical Association, a member of the U.S. Civil Service Commission, and president of the New York City Board of Police Commissioners.

In 1897, Roosevelt joined President William McKinley's administration (1897–1901) as assistant secretary of the navy. He supported war with Spain and strongly supported improving the navy for such a war. When the Spanish-American War (1898) began, Roosevelt resigned his post as assistant secretary and organized the First U.S. Volunteer Cavalry Regiment, commonly known as the Rough Riders. He was originally a lieutenant colonel but quickly became a full colonel. Roosevelt's actions as leader of the Rough Riders gained him a nomination for the Medal of Honor, though it was not approved. (Roosevelt was awarded the Medal of Honor posthumously in 2001—the only president ever to have received one.)

The returning hero was elected governor of New York in 1898. As he had in his previous public positions, Roosevelt took a strong stance against **corruption** and detested the awarding of political spoils. His zeal for reform angered local members of his own party. Many of them wanted Roosevelt to be added to the Republican national ticket in the upcoming election to get him out of New York.

PRESIDENCY

In the 1900 presidential election, Roosevelt was selected as William McKinley's running mate. They won, and Roosevelt enjoyed an uneventful vice presidency until the assassination of McKinley. On September 14, 1901, Roosevelt was sworn in as president at age 42, the youngest man to ever hold the office. Roosevelt gave the presidential home the name "the White House" and began bringing a different sort of guest to the mansion. A cowboy, naturalist, and thinker, he brought other cowboys, artists, writers, and even prizefighters to stay at the presidential home.

Fighting Corruption Roosevelt used his position of power to try to educate the public on the importance of rooting out corruption and establishing the United States in world affairs. He supported **antitrust** efforts that would take control of the economy away from a few very powerful business interests. Faced with a Congress that would not support progressive reforms, Roosevelt sought instead to improve foreign relations and work on wildlife conservation efforts.

Roosevelt himself wrote that he used every ounce of power the presidency afforded him. Not only did he believe in a strong executive but he also used the office as a means to explore the world and get the most from it. He enjoyed all the advantages that the power of the presidency gave him. Indeed, the president wrote:

> I declined to adopt the view that what was imperatively necessary for the Nation could not be done by the President unless he could find some specific authorization to do it. My belief was that it was not only his right but his duty to do anything that the needs of the Nation demanded unless such action was forbidden by the Constitution or by the law.

In 1902, Roosevelt personally intervened in a labor dispute between coal mines and miners. He used his influence to gain the cooperation of Wall Street in pressuring the parties to come to an agreement. Roosevelt invited both sides of the dispute to the White House so he could act as mediator. When the disagreement was resolved, the striking coal miners had achieved a raise in pay.

Square Deal In the 1904 campaign for the presidency, Roosevelt pushed what he called the Square Deal. The program would aid middle-class Americans by introducing regulation into the economy to break up monopolies and increase competition. In return, businesses would gain protection from unfair demands from workers. Roosevelt declared:

> We must act upon the motto of all for each and each for all. There must be ever present in our minds the fundamental truth that in a republic such as ours the only safety is to stand neither for nor against any man because he is rich or because he is poor, because he is engaged in one occupation or another, because he works with his brains or because he works with his hands. We must treat each man on his worth and merits as a man. We must see that each is given a square deal, because he is entitled to no more and should receive no less.

One of the major reforms passed under the Square Deal was the Hepburn Act of 1906. This act gave the Interstate Commerce Commission the power to set rates for railroad shipping across the country. This meant that railroads could not favor one business over another, making the commerce fairer for everyone.

Roosevelt supported the passage of the Pure Food and Drug Act of 1906, establishing laws for labeling food and its contents. He also supported the Meat Inspection Act, ensuring that meat would be properly inspected and processed in sanitary conditions to safeguard the public's health.

In addition to these laws, Roosevelt was the first president to see value in the conservation of national resources. He established the first National Bird Preserve in Florida. He founded the American Bison Society to try to prevent the extinction of the American bison. In 1905, he established the United States Forest Service and began establishing national forests, game preserves, and parks.

FINAL RUN FOR OFFICE

In 1908, Roosevelt's friend and secretary of war, William Howard Taft

HISTORY MAKERS

John Muir (1838–1914)

Considered the founder of the modern **conservation** and environmental movement, John Muir was born in Dunbar, Scotland, on April 21, 1838. When he was 11, his family moved from Scotland to Portage, Wisconsin. Even as a child, Muir loved the outdoors and was often seen hunting for birds' nests.

Once in the United States, Muir spent his days helping his family set up their new farm. He cleared woods and worked the plow, turning the wilderness into fields. It was hard work, which he claimed prepared him for his eventual life as a naturalist.

Muir was an inquisitive and highly imaginative teenager. His parents gave him special permission to read in the early morning, and he treasured these hours. He was also an inventor and able mechanic.

Because of his natural intelligence and self-study, Muir was accepted into the University of Wisconsin–Madison. He took a number of courses in the natural sciences but left in 1863 before graduating. Rather than return to the farm, Muir spent the next three years working as a mechanic. In 1867, an industrial accident nearly cost him his eyesight, and once he recovered, he decided that he would dedicate himself to seeing the world.

Muir's first trip was a thousand-mile walk from Indiana to Florida. His journal of the trip was published after his death in a book titled *A Thousand-Mile Walk to the Gulf*. In 1868, he visited Yosemite Valley in California. Muir traveled all over the West and Northwest but eventually settled back in Yosemite to live, work, and study. In 1876, Muir's interest in nature turned him into a political activist. He urged the federal government to establish national forest preserves.

In 1892, Muir established the Sierra Club. Its goal was to preserve the Sierra Nevada region. However, Muir's most influential work was with President Theodore Roosevelt (1901–1909). Muir took the president on a trip into Yosemite and convinced him of the need for federal control of natural parks. Roosevelt later established the country's system of national parks that remains today.

John Muir died on December 24, 1914, of pneumonia. In 2006, California governor Arnold Schwarzenegger inducted Muir into the California Hall of Fame. A number of parks, trails, and schools have been named in his honor.

(1909–1913), won the presidency. Roosevelt had strongly supported Taft for the high office but was unhappy with Taft's administration. Roosevelt decided to run again for president as a Republican in the election of 1912. When Taft won the nomination again, however, Roosevelt organized the Progressive, or Bull Moose, Party and became its presidential candidate. With the Republican Party split, Roosevelt and Taft lost to Democrat Woodrow Wilson (1913–1921).

In 1919, Roosevelt died in his sleep after a short illness, at the age of 60. He had written more than 26 books during his life and left behind a legacy of public works that continues to this day.

See also: Bull Moose Party; Conservation; McKinley, William; Progressive Reform; Pure Food and Drug Act; Taft, William Howard.

Further Reading

Garraty, John. *Teddy Roosevelt: American Rough Rider*. New York: Sterling, 2007.

Roosevelt, Theodore. *Theodore Roosevelt: An Autobiography*. New York: Dodo Press, 2006.

S

Seventeenth Amendment (1913)

A change added to the original U.S. Constitution that instituted a key progressive reform, the direct election of senators by the people of a state rather than by appointment by the state **legislature**. The Seventeenth Amendment also gives power to the governor of each state to appoint a senator, if an opening occurs, until an election can take place.

CONSTITUTIONAL ORIGINS

In 1789, the U.S. Constitution established the legislative branch of the government, which consists of two houses, the House of Representatives and the Senate. Each member of the House of Representatives represents a district in his or her state. The number of representatives in each state is dependent upon that state's population, meaning that states with large populations have more representatives than states with small populations. Each state also has two senators, regardless of that state's population.

Because the framers of the Constitution were cautious about **democracy** in government and wanted a balance within the legislative branch, they decided that, while members of the House of Representatives could be directly elected by the people of their states, the members of the Senate should be elected by state legislatures. The framers felt that because senators would not have to worry about reelection and trying to win the popular vote, they could better focus on the nation's issues.

LIMITING DEMOCRACY?

With the start of the **Progressive** movement in the United States in the 1890s, this method of appointing senators, which seemed undemocratic, began to be seriously questioned by the American public. Progressive leaders argued for reform in all aspects of government, which included allowing citizens to have greater participation in their government.

Progressives argued that state legislatures were often controlled by corrupt leaders who looked out for their own interests and did not represent the best interests of the people. Sometimes, state legislatures could not agree upon a candidate, resulting in no Senate appointments at all.

Progressive Republican senators Robert La Follette of Wisconsin and George Norris of Nebraska strongly supported direct election of senators by the **electorate**. Every year, from 1893 to 1902, a constitutional **amendment** to elect senators by popular vote was proposed in Congress, but most members of the Senate rejected it.

Investigative journalists, nicknamed "muckrakers" by President Theodore Roosevelt (1901–1909) because of their role in digging up the

Electing Our Senators

In 1913, the Seventeenth Amendment was added to the U.S. Constitution. During the Progressive Era of the early 1900s, it was one of a number of amendments added to the Constitution to improve the social and political aspects of American society and give more rights to American citizens.

The Seventeenth Amendment allows for direct election of senators by the people of a state rather than by state legislatures. It replaced the phrase "chosen by the Legislature thereof" with "elected by the people thereof" in the first paragraph of Article I, Section 3, of the Constitution. The Seventeenth Amendment also allows the governor of each state to appoint a senator if an opening occurs, until an election can take place.

> The Senate of the United States shall be composed of two Senators from each State, elected by the people thereof, for six years; and each Senator shall have one vote. The electors in each State shall have the qualifications requisite for electors of the most numerous branch of the State legislatures.
>
> When vacancies happen in the representation of any State in the Senate, the executive authority of each State shall issue writs of election to fill such vacancies: *Provided*, That the legislature of any State may empower the executive thereof to make temporary appointments until the people fill the vacancies by election as the legislature may direct.
>
> This amendment shall not be so construed as to affect the election or term of any Senator chosen before it becomes valid as part of the Constitution.

"muck," or dirt, of American society, also tried to influence the direct election of senators. In 1906, muckraking journalist David Graham Phillips (1867–1911) wrote a series of articles for *Cosmopolitan* magazine called "The Treason of the Senate," in which senators were portrayed as taking bribes from industrialists and financiers. It was this article that led to President Roosevelt publicly denouncing muckrakers in a speech, but there was no denying their influence on the American public.

Before **ratification** of the Seventeenth Amendment, however, many states had changed their own laws so that voters had more influence over the selection of senators. Voters participating in **primary elections** designated their preference for one of the parties' candidates for a senatorial seat. Usually, the state legislatures supported the people's preference. By 1912, 29 states were nominating senators on some type of popular basis. In 1911, Senator Joseph Bristow from Kansas proposed an amendment to the Constitution. Those senators who had been chosen only by their respective state legislatures fought against the bill. Ultimately, however, the majority of the Senate approved the bill because of the vote of those senators who had been chosen by the state legislatures with the guidance of the preference system.

RATIFICATION

After the Senate passed the bill, the House passed it in the summer of 1912. Finally it was sent to the states for ratification. Connecticut became the 36th state to ratify the Seventeenth Amendment in April 1913, giving the amendment the required three-fourths majority necessary to be added to the Constitution. The following year, all elections for senator were held by popular vote.

See also: La Follete, Robert; Muckrakers; Norris, George W.

Sherman Antitrust Act (1890)

The first law passed by the U.S. Congress to prohibit abusive **trusts** and **monopolies**. In 1890, a Republican senator from Ohio, John Sherman, introduced an **antitrust** bill into Congress. Speaking against monopolies, Sherman noted that these powerful companies:

> ... control the market, raise or lower prices, as will best promote its selfish interests, reduce prices in a particular locality and break down competition and advance prices at will where competition does not exist. ... The law of selfishness, uncontrolled by competition, compels it to disregard the interest of the consumer.

DEMANDS FOR REGULATION

During the last quarter of the nineteenth century, many industries–iron and steel, oil, farm machinery, flour, sugar, and meat, for example–grew bigger, organized into **corporations**, and merged. Some of the most aggressive entrepreneurs, such as John D. Rockefeller in oil refining, managed to establish monopolies or near monopolies. In 1880, Rockefeller's

Standard Oil Trust controlled more than 90 percent of the oil refining in the country. In fact, the trend in almost all industries was toward increasing size and establishing control of an industry through monopoly.

Growth of Big Business The success or failure of a business depended upon several factors. Among these were shrewd and efficient management, elimination of competition through purchase or ruthless practices, and possession of **patents**. As companies prospered, they swallowed up or drove their competitors out of business and formed larger and larger business combinations. As Rockefeller noted, by saving the wastes of competition the big corporations had "revolutionized the way of doing business all over the world," and he insisted that this type of business practice was "here to stay."

The new, big corporations produced great quantities of goods, and when they were well run, they could produce more goods at less cost than small businesses. The reduced costs, however, were not necessarily passed on to consumers. Profits of these businesses could be huge, as they were for Rockefeller. Good business leaders poured much of their income back into their businesses to make them still bigger.

Survival of the Fittest Many Americans admired and envied these leaders of big businesses. They proved a theory, known as survival of the fittest, was becoming increasingly popular. Some Americans, especially farmers, workers, and small-business owners, feared the growing power of the big corporations because they were able to control wages and prices. Furthermore, they drove competitors out of business and pressured the U.S. government to pass legislation that was favorable to their interests.

At the time, few Americans wanted to eliminate big business, but many wanted the huge trusts, these powerful corporations, brought under some type of control. Many people believed this was the only way to restore competition and economic opportunity in the United States. By the late 1880s, public opinion on the issue of regulating, or controlling, big business grew stronger. In the election of 1888, both the Republican and Democratic parties agreed on this issue and voiced opposition to monopolies in their **platforms**.

In particular, the public focused on the business practices of the Standard Oil Trust. In the public mind, the term *trust* had come to mean, not just a trust in the legal sense (as a form of business organization), but any business that was so powerful that it could influence the general level of production and prices.

PASSAGE OF THE ACT

In response to the public outcry against the trusts, John Sherman introduced a bill that would become known as the Sherman Antitrust Act. Passed in July 1890, the act forbade every contract, combination, or conspiracy in restraint of trade and provided that anyone who entered into such an agreement would be subject to a fine of $1,000 or a year in prison or both.

While the act seemed to meet the demand of **progressive** reformers, it was ineffective. It did distinguish between desirable or unavoidable monopolies and other businesses, but it proved to be unenforceable. For many years, in the lawsuits brought by the government, the courts almost always ruled against the government. Few "combinations in restraint of trade" were dissolved. Later, additional legislation passed by Congress was more successful in breaking up trusts, now illegal in the United States.

See also: Social Darwinism; Social Justice; Tarbell, Ida; Veblen, Thorstein.

Further Reading

Cefrey, Holly. *The Sherman Antitrust Act: Getting Big Business Under Control.* New York: Rosen Publishing, 2003.

McNeese, Tim. *The Robber Barons and the Sherman Antitrust Act: Reshaping American Business.* New York: Chelsea House, 2008.

Sinclair, Upton (1878–1968)

American writer, political activist, and social reformer. Upton Sinclair was the author of more than 90 books in the first half of the twentieth century. In 1943, he won the sought-after Pulitzer Prize for his novel *Dragon's Teeth*. Yet Sinclair's most famous work is the **muckraking** novel *The Jungle,* written in 1906. Though fiction, *The Jungle* exposed the terrible working conditions in Chicago's meatpacking plants and contributed to the establishment of new food regulation laws in the United States.

Upton Sinclair was born in Baltimore, Maryland, in 1878 but moved to New York City when he was 10. His family was poor, and at the age of 15, Sinclair began to support himself by writing adventure tales for various boys' weekly magazines. Sinclair wrote several novels between 1901 and 1904 but never made much money from them.

In 1904, Sinclair read about a strike at a meatpacking plant in Chicago and decided this would be the plot of his next novel. For a few months, Sinclair visited the Chicago stockyards, talking to **immigrant** workers. He witnessed their grueling 12-hour-a-day schedule and the horrible conditions in which they worked. Based on his experiences in Chicago, Sinclair began writing *The Jungle.*

The story of *The Jungle* centers on a Lithuanian immigrant named Jurgis Rudkus. Rudkus arrives in America with dreams of wealth and opportunity. He finds work at a meatpacking plant in a place Sinclair called "Packingtown." Soon Rudkus's life falls apart after he is unable to support his family and ultimately becomes a criminal. At the end of the novel, Rudkus dreams of hope again by joining the **Socialist Party**.

The Jungle was first published in serial form by the socialist newspaper *The Appeal to Reason*. It was rejected by five publishing companies until Doubleday agreed to publish it as a novel in February 1906. It became an immediate best seller. Though Sinclair's main goal of the book was to attack **capitalism** and evoke sympathy for immigrant workers, most

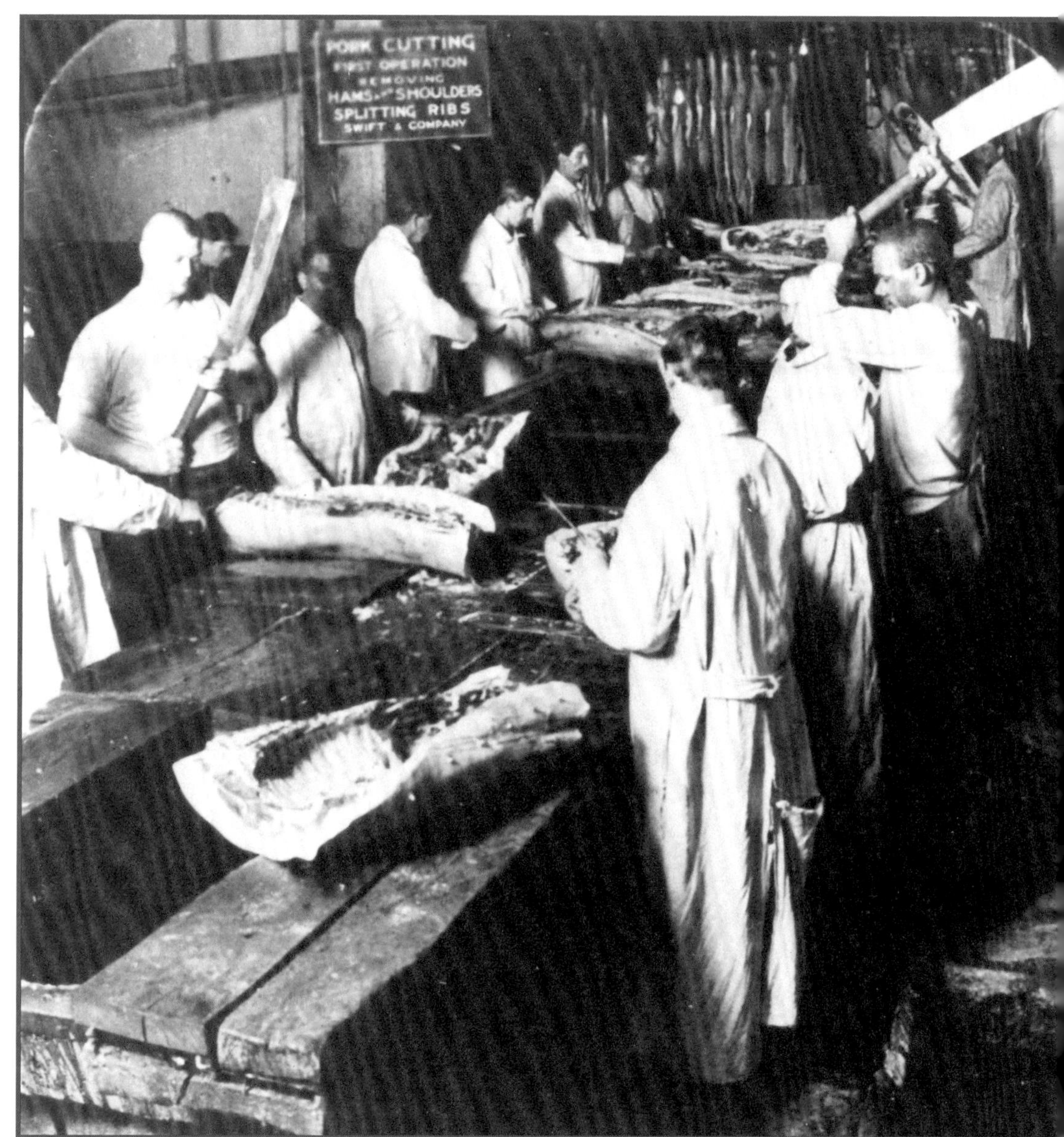

A 1904 photograph shows butchers carving carcasses in the unsanitary conditions of meat-packing plants of the time. Upton Sinclair's novel, *The Jungle,* vividly described the unsafe and filthy workplaces in which meat was prepared. Readers of the novel, including President Theodore Roosevelt, were appalled.

readers were astonished and horrified by his descriptions of the meat-packing plants. Sinclair described how dead rats were shoveled into sausage-grinding machines and how meat inspectors were bribed to approve diseased cows for use as meat. As Sinclair later described it, "I aimed at the public's heart and by accident I hit it in the stomach."

The Jungle had one of the greatest impacts on American society since Harriet Beecher Stowe's abolitionist novel *Uncle Tom's Cabin* (1852). Within months, the public demanded reforms in the American meat industry. President Theodore Roosevelt (1901–1909) sent agents to Chicago to determine whether the meatpacking plants were as bad as Sinclair described and found that they were actually much worse. By June of 1906, Congress had passed the Pure Food and Drug Act, which set federal standards for all packaged food and drugs, and the Meat Inspection Act, which called for federal inspection of all meat-processing plants.

Although Upton Sinclair never again achieved the popular success of *The Jungle*, he continued to write many more novels through the 1950s. Sinclair remained a political activist throughout his life. In 1934, he ran as the Democratic candidate for governor of California, and nearly won. He died in 1948 at the age of 90.

See also: Food and Drug Act, Pure; Muckrakers; Roosevelt, Theodore; *The Jungle*, in the "Viewpoints" Section.

Further Reading

Arthur, Anthony. *Radical Innocent: Upton Sinclair.* New York: Random House, 2006.

Sinclair, Upton. *The Jungle.* New York: Simon and Schuster, 2004.

Sixteenth Amendment (1913)

A change added to the original U.S. Constitution that allowed Congress to tax the income of individuals without regard to the population of each state. The income tax was a key element of progressive reforms because it was seen as a way for the government to raise money to help the less fortunate in society.

The original Constitution, adopted in 1789, allowed for Congress to ". . . lay and collect taxes, duties, imposts, and excises, pay the Debts and provide for the common Defense and general Welfare of the United States. . . ." The Constitution also stated that "No . . . direct . . . Tax shall be laid, unless in Proportion to the Census. . . ." This meant that any tax imposed by the federal government had to be based on each state's population, so that people who lived in states with larger populations would have to pay a higher percentage of taxes.

However, until the 1860s, Americans paid few taxes. The federal government was usually able to support itself from taxes on goods brought into the country. The cost of the Civil War (1861–1865) changed that, requiring additional measures for raising money. In 1861, Congress passed the Revenue Act. For the first time, Americans were asked to pay a tax on their income. The Revenue Act, which went into effect in 1862, required Americans who earned more than $800 a year to pay a 3 percent tax, and those who earned more than $10,000 to pay a 5 percent tax.

Once the Civil War ended in 1865, there was no longer a need for an income tax, and it was abolished in 1872. Yet, at the same time, American **Progressives** began to support a graduated income tax, or an income tax based on how much people earned, in place of high **tariffs**, or taxes on imported goods. Many people felt that it was fairest to ask those who earned the most money to pay the highest tax rates.

In 1894, Congress passed the Revenue Act, which reduced U.S. tariff rates and, to make up for the loss, established a 2 percent tax on incomes of more than $4,000 a year. This income tax was quickly challenged because it was not apportioned according to the population of each state. In 1895, the U.S. Supreme Court ruled this federal income tax to be unconstitutional. Once again, the federal government was forced to rely on tariffs for its revenue. However, Congress continued to debate the issue of the income tax. Progressives argued that high tariffs often fell disproportionately on less wealthy Americans. Yet each time an income tax was introduced in Congress, conservative Republicans in the Senate rejected it.

Finally, in 1909, President William Howard Taft (1909–1913) proposed a constitutional **amendment** to allow for federal income taxes on individuals. Ultimately, Congress agreed upon the establishment of an **excise tax,** or a tax on goods produced within the country, as well as a constitutional amendment to allow the federal government to impose an income tax without regard to the states' populations.

The Income Tax

In 1913, the Sixteenth Amendment was added to the U.S. Constitution. During the Progressive Era of the 1900s, it was one of a number of amendments that sought to improve many social and political aspects of American society.

The Sixteenth Amendment authorized Congress to establish an income tax on individuals without regard to the population of each state. Progressives argued that it was fairest for those Americans who earned the most money to pay the highest tax rates in the United States.

After the passage of the Sixteenth Amendment, Congress passed the Revenue Act of 1913, which officially established a federal income tax. Form 1040 was introduced as the standard tax-reporting form, which, though it has gone through many changes, is still in use today. At the time, less than one percent of the population paid income tax. The Act reads:

> The Congress shall have power to lay and collect taxes on incomes, from whatever source derived, without apportionment among the several States, and without regard to any census or enumeration.

S

By 1913, 36 states had **ratified** the Sixteenth Amendment to the Constitution, giving it the required three-fourths majority necessary to be added to the Constitution. That year, Congress passed the Revenue Act of 1913, which established a federal income tax and lowered tariff rates. Today, the federal government relies on the income tax as its primary source of revenue.

See also: Payne-Aldrich Tariff Act.

Social Darwinism

The application of English **naturalist** Charles Darwin's ideas about **evolution** to society and business. During the **Progressive** Era, to justify its often unpopular actions, big business conveniently drew on the views of philosophers and scientists.

In 1859, Charles Darwin, who lived from 1809 to 1882, published his influential book *On the Origin of Species by Means of Natural Selection, or the Preservation of the Favored Races in the Struggle for Life.* In this and in later books, Darwin attempted to prove that, in nature, those plants and animals that survive do so because they are the fittest.

This doctrine, known as the survival of the fittest, was also held by Herbert Spencer, another Englishman who developed an economic theory of extreme **laissez-faire**, or no government regulation of business. Spencer, who lived from 1820 until 1903, believed that those who got ahead deserved to do so because they had proven themselves the strongest, or the fittest. Darwin's theory matched Spencer's philosophy. Therefore, in civilized society, some held, just as in nature, those who survive are the fittest.

Followers of Darwin and Spencer believed in this doctrine so firmly that they combined the two philosophies into what they considered a **natural law**. Among prominent Americans who advocated Social Darwinism was a Yale University professor, William Graham Sumner, who wrote:

> . . . We cannot go outside of this alternative: liberty, inequality, survival of the fittest; not liberty, equality, survival of the unfittest. The former carries society forward and favors all its best members; the latter carries society downwards and favors all its worst members.

According to Sumner, the weak fall prey to the strong in the struggle for existence. Thus, business tycoons, the "fittest" members of society, reap material riches because they deserve them—as the products of natural selection.

DEFENDING BIG BUSINESS

Social Darwinism became a dominant American philosophy during the last part of the nineteenth century. It seemed to support the system that produced the multimillionaires who grew to dominate big business, such as John D. Rockefeller of Standard Oil and Andrew Carnegie of U.S. Steel. These men and other business leaders readily accepted this philosophy.

This was especially true of Carnegie, who from an early age had questioned his Christian faith. After reading Spencer's books, Carnegie wrote, "Light came in as a flood and all was clear." Rockefeller, a devout Baptist, told his Sunday-school class that:

> . . . growth of a large business is merely survival of the fittest . . . This is not an evil tendency in business. It is merely the working-out of a law of nature and of God.

As Spencer had argued, Rockefeller also believed the government should not interfere with the natural evolution of business and should not restrain business through regulation and reform. On the other hand, those in big business believed it was fine for the government to favor industry with laws such as protective **tariffs**.

Social Darwinism was not only the creed of big business. It was also widely accepted throughout the United States in the last part of the nineteenth century.

REJECTION OF SOCIAL DARWINISM

Many Americans–including farmers, labor leaders, and advocates of progressive reform–refused to accept a social philosophy based on social Darwinism. Believing that the benefits of society belong to all its members, many people continued to press for reforms. During the last decade of the nineteenth century and the early twentieth century, the efforts of reformers were increasingly successful, and the influence of social Darwinism declined.

See also: Roosevelt, Theodore; Sherman Antitrust Act; Veblen, Thorstein.

Further Reading

Crook, Paul. *Darwin's Coat-Tails: Essays on Social Darwinism.* New York: Peter Lang Publishing, 2007.

Dickens, Peter. *Social Darwinism: Linking Evolutionary Thought to Social Theory.* London: Open University Press, 2000.

Social Justice

The concept that all people are entitled to fair treatment, decent working conditions, and the essentials of life, such as food, clothing, and shelter. Achieving social justice in the United States was a major goal of the nineteenth-century **Progressive** movement.

S

SOCIAL INJUSTICES

In 1900, the average workweek for industrial workers was about 60 hours. The average rate of pay was under $10 a week, and unskilled workers earned even less. Working conditions and pay varied little from one industry to another. For example, even though coal mining was an industry in which workers often faced severe hardship, miners received no higher pay than those in other industries. The average coal miner worked 10 hours a day and earned about $400 a year. When the mines shut down for several days or even weeks, the miners received no pay. Mining was particularly dangerous and unpleasant. A miner in the late 1900s wrote:

> Day in and day out, from Monday morning to Saturday evening, between the rising and the setting of the sun, I am in the underground workings of the coal mines. From the seams the water trickles into the ditches along the gangways; if not water, it is the gas which can hurl us into eternity . . .

Living Conditions Prices were low in the early 1900s, but so were wages. Even with the low prices of the times, a worker's earnings were often not enough to meet basic family needs. A family with several children, for example, usually lived on the edge of poverty. If a worker were injured on the job, the family would likely receive no income at all. Debts would then pile up, and sometimes families could not recover from their losses. Families who made just enough money to survive were in serious trouble when illness or unemployment struck. In the early 1900s, most workers and their families lived constantly with these fears.

Women and Children By 1900, about 5 million women were in the American labor force. Some worked in offices or stores and many taught school. Most unskilled women held factory jobs where they received less pay than men for the same work.

Among the children under the age of 16 working in 1900, fewer than half were employed in industry. Yet factory work was generally the hardest type of work for children. They were required to stay indoors in the factory and usually did the same repetitive task for hours at a time. The textile industry hired the most children. Muckraking writer John Spargo exposed some of the abusive practices of big industries. Spargo reported on the working conditions in the textile mills; he described children who worked nights and had to be kept awake by having cold water splashed on their faces. He also told of the physical effects of hard labor on children, noting that "they are usually behind other children in height, weight, and girth of chest,–often as much as two or three years."

Immigrants **Immigration** to the United States reached its peak in the early twentieth century. At least 750,000 people arrived in the United States each year between 1905 and 1914. Most of these immigrants came from Italy, Greece, Poland, Russia, and the Middle East.

Once admitted to the United States, most immigrants at the time faced years of hard work for low pay in the factories of New York, the coal mines of Pennsylvania, or the meatpacking houses of Chicago and other Midwestern cities. While some were defeated by poverty and prejudice, most newcomers took on the struggle in order to attain a better life.

Most immigrants came to the United States to find new economic opportunities. Many, however, were unable to find steady work for several reasons–lack of skills, language difficulties, and prejudice. In general, immigrants had to take those jobs that offered the longest hours and the lowest pay.

Many newcomers worked as peddlers or in **tenement** sweatshops—small clothing industries where people worked in unsanitary and unsafe conditions. A magazine reporter described the sweatshops of New York City:

> In the tenement "sweatshops" unhealthy and unclean conditions are almost universal, and those of filth and contagion common. The employes [sic] are in the main foreign-born and newly arrived. The proportion of female labor is large, and child labor is largely used. Wages are from a fourth to a third less than in the larger shops. As to hours, there is no limit except the endurance of the employes [sic] . . . the hours of labor being rarely less than twelve, generally thirteen or fourteen, frequently fifteen to eighteen.

Poverty forced the immigrants to live in the most inexpensive city housing available—the tenements. In general, these buildings were unsafe and unhealthy. Noise, filth, and confusion were characteristic of immigrant neighborhoods. Some immigrant families sought better apartments. High rents and low wages, however, made it almost impossible for them to improve their living conditions.

African Americans Despite the push for social justice during the Progressive Era, little improvement was made in the lives of African Americans. Their hopes for sharing in Theodore Roosevelt's (1901–1909) Square Deal were quickly dashed. Roosevelt wrote "the only wise and honorable and Christian thing to do is to treat each black man and each white man strictly on his merits as a man." Later, Roosevelt risked outrage while speaking to a heavily armed crowd in Butte, Montana, during his 1903 Western tour:

> I fought beside colored troops at Santiago [Cuba], and I hold that if a man is good enough to be put up and shot at then he is good enough for me to do what I can to get him a square deal.

Despite Roosevelt's personal views, the federal government did little to help African Americans achieve racial equality. In the South, racial tensions increased. Some politicians deliberately used the race issue to win elections; **lynching** was common throughout much of the South. Furthermore, violence against African Americans was not confined to the South. In 1908, for example, a bloody race riot occurred in Springfield, the state capital of Illinois, and, ironically, the birthplace of Abraham Lincoln.

Before 1900, African Americans in the South had made some strides in education, largely as a result of aid from private groups. Yet it soon became evident that further progress would come only if the states also gave their support. During the Progressive Era, however, few state governments attempted to help improve education for African Americans. African Americans continued to lack political power and to be **segregated** from white Americans. During this time, the economic conditions of African Americans improved little, if at all.

THE SOCIAL JUSTICE MOVEMENT The settlement houses first established in the 1890s became the centers of the social justice movement during the Progressive Era. The movement was an organized effort by social workers to rid American cities of some of their worst problems. At first, the influence of the social workers did not reach beyond the slums in which they worked. Business leaders and politicians paid little attention to their calls for **reform**.

By 1900, however, social workers were being heard. They had begun to investigate social problems and assemble revealing facts and data about those problems. They organized themselves more efficiently than before, and some began to devote their energies to the care of immigrants. Other social workers became concerned with the problems of labor. As a result of their efforts, laws were passed to ensure and carry out reforms.

Jane Addams and Hull House During a tour of Europe in the late 1880s, Jane Addams decided to devote her life to helping the poor. She visited Toynbee Hall, a settlement house located in the slums of London, England. She returned home to the United States to establish a similar house. On September 18, 1889, Jane Addams opened Hull House in Chicago on Halstead Street, a long thoroughfare teeming with immigrants. Addams planned for Hull House to be a center for poor workers and immigrants.

A wide variety of social and cultural activities were available at Hull House. Children played there, and older people sought companionship. Unemployed men could find a meal and a bed. Art and sewing classes were set up. Kindergartens were established, and medical care was made available.

Addams's success and influence grew and became increasingly widespread. She and other settlement house workers began speaking out and writing about social problems, calling for reform, for changes that would improve the quality of life. The movement for social justice owed much to the efforts of Jane Addams. As the historian Henry Steele Commager wrote:

> Over the years Jane Addams built a bridge between the immigrants and the old-stock Americans, between the working classes and the immigrants, between the amateur reformers and the professional politicians, between private philanthropy [charity] and government.

Housing The muckraking photojournalist Jacob Riis, whose words and images exposed the horrors of slum living, was the first reformer to seriously interest the American people in the problems of slum housing. His 1890 book, *How the Other Half Lives*, attracted nationwide attention. Readers of his books began to call for reform, and their outcries led to the first organized efforts to wipe out slums in American cities.

In New York State in the late 1890s, then-governor Theodore Roosevelt appointed a Tenement Housing Commission. Its work led to the passage of the Tenement House Law of 1901. This state law did away with certain types of tenements that were first built in New York City in 1879. Reformers had criticized these early buildings because they were so close together that they prevented adequate air and light.

Throughout the Progressive Era, Jacob Riis and many other reformers battled against the slums. These reformers were convinced that better housing was the key to solving other urban problems, such as crime and disease. After 1900, state after state passed laws regulating housing. Most reforms began in large cities. In general, the reforms required that slum landlords improve buildings by providing fire escapes, additional sanitary facilities, and better heating and lighting. Although the slums were not wiped out during the Progressive Era, some of the worst features of tenement living were improved.

Concern for Children One of the chief concerns of the social justice movement was child welfare. Children living in tenements had no place to play other than the streets and filthy alleys. Their health was often damaged by the unsanitary conditions of the slum environment. In addition, many worked long hours beginning at an early age.

A key goal of social reformers was to seek legislation that restricted child labor. Reformers also made efforts to improve the neighborhoods in which children lived. For example, in her book *The Spirit of Youth and the City Streets*, Jane Addams presented an argument for play areas for children. Soon after 1900, most large cities began providing parks and playgrounds for them. By 1915, more than 400 cities had opened such playgrounds.

Still another concern of social workers was the lack of medical treatment available to children who lived in the slums. As Jane Addams wrote:

> . . . The first three crippled children we encountered in the neighborhood had all been injured while their mothers were at work; one had fallen out of a third-story window, another had been burned, and the third had a curved spine due to the fact that for three years he had been tied all day long to the leg of the kitchen table. . . .

People were aroused to action by this kind of information. As a result, free clinics and day-care nurseries were established in some cities. In some districts, free milk was distributed to children, and some public schools began medical and dental examinations to determine if children had health problems.

Protection of Women Workers Reformers seeking social justice fought to limit the working hours of women in the nation's factories. In 1908, the U.S. Supreme Court ruled that legislation limiting women's hours of work was constitutional. By the end of the

Progressive Era, most states had either passed such laws or strengthened existing ones.

Women workers usually received less pay than men received for the same jobs. Reformers across the country called for minimum wage laws for women. In 1912, Massachusetts became the first state to establish a committee to recommend minimum wages for women. While some states followed this example, most did not.

OTHER SOCIAL LEGISLATION

During the Progressive Era, other important social legislation was passed by the states. Some states passed laws that provided aid for the elderly. A few states passed laws that provided assistance for widowed and divorced mothers. Because many of the child labor laws were difficult to enforce at the workplace, reformers urged that the legal age at which children could leave school be raised.

Legislation that improved social justice for all people was one of the most important contributions of the reformers known as the Progressives. Throughout the 1920s, many states extended the new laws, and most states improved the enforcement of existing laws. Perhaps most important, the Progressives had established the basis for further social reforms, many of which would take place during the 1930s and beyond.

See also: Addams, Jane; Child Labor; Hull House; Muckrakers; Riis, Jacob; Roosevelt, Theodore; Sinclair, Upton.

Further Reading

Dudley, William. *Social Justice.* Farmington Hills, Mich.: Greenhaven Press, 2005.

McNeese, Tim. *The Progressive Movement: Advocating Social Change.* New York: Chelsea House, 2007.

Stanton, Elizabeth Cady (1815–1902)

American **progressive** reformer, feminist, suffragist, and leader in the women's rights movement. Elizabeth Cady Stanton was born on November 13, 1815, in Johnstown, New York. Her father was an attorney and New York Supreme Court justice. From him, Elizabeth learned about the law and gained an interest in public life.

EARLY LIFE

In 1830, Cady attended the Troy Female Seminary. She graduated in 1832 with one of the best educations available to women of her day. Following her formal education, she began reading law in her father's offices and conversing with his law clerks. Through a self-directed study of her father's law books, she came to understand how biased the law was against women, who could own virtually nothing and had no rights, even to their own children. Abused wives were advised to endure their treatment because there was no legal recourse.

Elizabeth's cousin Gerrit Smith had a great influence on her life. It was at Smith's house where she was introduced to the **abolitionist** movement. Although the Cadys owned slaves, it was not until Elizabeth met fugitive slaves and antislavery activists that she took an interest and active role in abolitionism. It was also through Smith that she met Henry Stanton. In 1840, Elizabeth and Henry were married. Elizabeth insisted that the ceremony be altered, as she would not promise to "obey" her husband.

SPEAKING OUT

The Stantons traveled to London to attend the World Anti-Slavery Convention. Stanton was outraged when a number of women were denied entry to the convention, notably Lucretia Mott. This led her from the abolitionist movement to the women's rights movement with Mott. She began speaking out in favor of women's rights and led a campaign in New York for married women to be granted property rights.

In the summer of 1848, Stanton again met with Lucretia Mott, near Seneca Falls. They decided to organize the first women's rights convention on July 19. Stanton became the recognized leader of the movement with her presentation of the Declaration of Sentiments. Modeled after the Declaration of Independence, Stanton's paper outlined the injustices suffered by women in the United States and called for equal voting rights for women. The Declaration of Sentiments begins:

> When, in the course of human events, it becomes necessary for one portion of the family of man to assume among the people of the earth a position different from that which they have hitherto occupied, but one to which the laws of nature and of nature's God entitle them, a decent respect to the opinions of mankind requires that they should declare the causes that impel them to such a course.
>
> We hold these truths to be self-evident: that all men and women are created equal; that they are endowed by their Creator with certain inalienable rights; that among these are life, liberty, and the pursuit of happiness; that to secure these rights governments are instituted, deriving their just powers from the consent of the governed.

Even among women, the idea of equal voting rights for women was controversial, although the convention eventually approved the declaration.

A second women's rights convention was then held in Rochester, New York. Along with Susan B. Anthony, Stanton traveled the country giving talks before legislatures and conventions. She wrote articles, essays, pamphlets, and speeches.

During the Civil War (1861–1865), Stanton again took up the banner of abolitionism. However, when activists seeking equal rights for blacks would not support equal rights for women, Stanton abandoned her efforts to help them.

In 1869, Stanton helped to found the National Woman Suffrage Association. Compared to the American Woman Suffrage Association, Stanton's organization was more radical. Eventually, the organizations merged in an effort to consolidate power.

Stanton remained more radical than others in the women's rights movement. She wrote essays on religion and strove to prove that

HISTORY MAKERS

Jeanette Rankin (1880–1973)

Born in Montana in 1880, Jeanette Rankin graduated from Montana State University with a Bachelor of Science degree in biology. She worked as a schoolteacher and briefly as a social worker. By 1910, Rankin had become involved in the woman suffrage movement, or the campaign to give women the right to vote.

Rankin moved to New York and worked for the New York Woman Suffrage Party. In March 1913, she was one of thousands of suffragists to march in a suffrage parade in Washington, D.C. Rankin then returned to Montana to help women in that state gain the right to vote, which was granted in 1914. Two years later, Rankin ran as a Republican for a seat in the U.S. House of Representatives. She won, becoming the first woman elected to the U.S. Congress.

In Congress, Rankin continued to work for women's rights. In 1917, she opened the debate in Congress on the Susan B. Anthony Amendment, which would give all women the right to vote. This ultimately became the Nineteenth Amendment, which was **ratified** by the states in 1920.

Rankin remained in Congress for one term, and then, in 1939, ran for Congress again. This time when elected, she was one of eight women in Congress. She served just one term because her antiwar stance made her unpopular. For the rest of her life, Rankin worked for peace and women's rights. She died in 1973 at the age of 92.

scripture could support women's rights as much as it had been used to deny those rights. She wrote *The Woman's Bible* as a treatise on this stance against the oppression of organized Christianity.

Stanton worked for women's rights throughout her life. She died on October 26, 1902. Women did not gain the right to vote until 1920, 18 years after her death.

Further Reading

Stanton, Elizabeth Cady. *The Woman's Bible: A Classic Feminist Perspective*. Mineola, N.Y.: Dover Publications, 2003.

Ward, Geoffrey. *Not For Ourselves Alone: The Story of Elizabeth Cady Stanton and Susan B. Anthony*. New York: Knopf, 2001.

Suffragists

People who worked for woman suffrage, or the right to vote. Most suffragist leaders were women, but a significant number of men also supported this powerful movement.

The start of the woman suffrage movement and the first American suffragists are usually traced back to the Seneca Falls Convention for women's rights in Seneca Falls, New York, in 1848. It was the first women's rights convention held in the United States. The Seneca Falls Convention was hosted by Elizabeth Cady Stanton and Lucretia Mott, women who also supported the **abolitionist**, or antislavery, movement but who had realized that in order for women to have any political authority in the United States they needed an equal rights movement of their own.

At the convention, Stanton presented the Declaration of Sentiments—a document modeled on the Declaration of Independence (1776)—which called for equal rights for women in American society, including the right to vote. In 1869, Stanton, along with notable suffragist Susan B. Anthony, formed the National Woman Suffrage Association. This group believed that their focus should center on women's right to vote above other issues. At the same time, other women's rights activists, including Lucy Stone and African American abolitionist Frederick Douglass, formed the American Woman Suffrage Association. This group focused on gaining the right to vote for all Americans, including women and African Americans. Later, in 1890, under Stanton's leadership, the two groups merged to form the National American Woman Suffrage Association.

In 1878, Susan B. Anthony and Elizabeth Cady Stanton wrote a Woman Suffrage Amendment to the U.S. Constitution, which became known as the Anthony Amendment. It would finally pass, worded exactly the same, in 1920 as the Nineteenth Amendment, giving American women the right to vote.

By the early years of the twentieth century, some suffragist leaders favored more radical approaches to gaining the vote. In 1913, Alice Paul, who had been a member of the National American Woman Suffrage Association, and Lucy Burns organized the Congressional Union for Women Suffrage, which three years later became known as the National Women's Party. Paul and other members of the National Woman's Party participated in hunger strikes, picketed the White House, and organized demonstrations to publicize the cause for woman suffrage.

Another important suffragist, Carrie Chapman Catt, was chosen by Anthony to succeed her as president of the National American Woman Suffrage Association in 1900. Catt did not support Alice Paul's radical tactics. Instead she favored lobbying lawmakers in Congress to push for the woman suffrage amendment. At the time of Catt's presidency, the National American Woman Suffrage Association had become the largest and most important suffrage association in the United States. Catt and her supporters noted that the United States was fighting World War I (1914–1918) "to make the world safe for **democracy**," yet hundreds of thousands of the nation's adult citizens could not vote. It was through her work that President Woodrow Wilson (1913–1921) was won over to the idea of woman suffrage by 1918. Indeed, on September 30, 1918, Wilson addressed the U.S. Senate, urging them to pass the proposed amendment. The president noted,

> GENTLEMEN OF THE SENATE: The unusual circumstances of a world war in which we stand and are judged . . . will, I hope, justify in your thought, as it does in

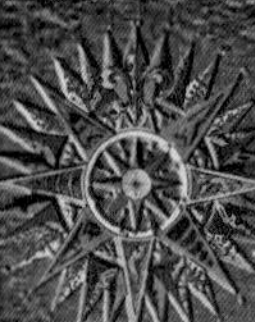

Woman Suffrage in the United States Before 1919

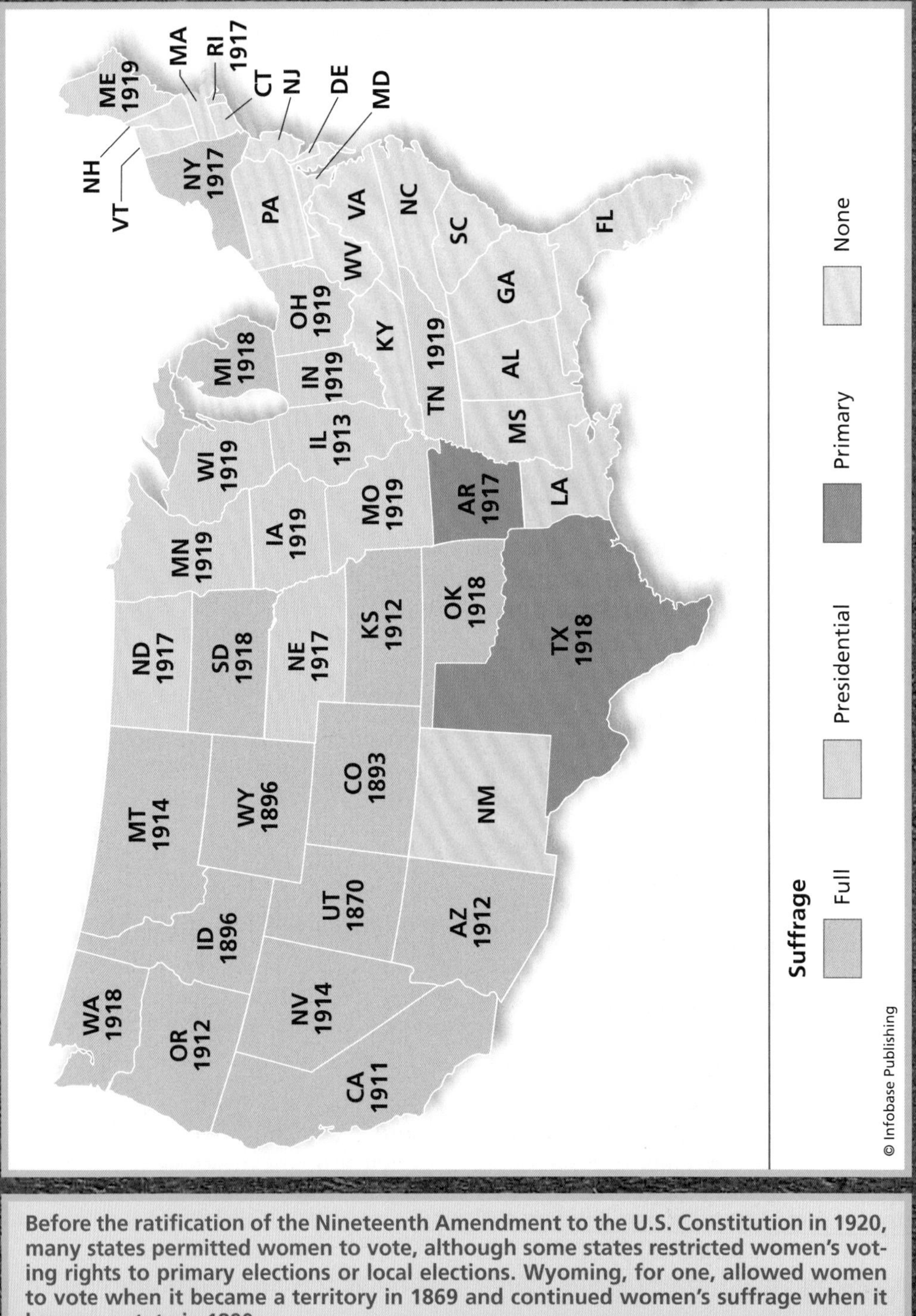

© Infobase Publishing

Before the ratification of the Nineteenth Amendment to the U.S. Constitution in 1920, many states permitted women to vote, although some states restricted women's voting rights to primary elections or local elections. Wyoming, for one, allowed women to vote when it became a territory in 1869 and continued women's suffrage when it became a state in 1890.

From Jeanette Rankin to Hillary Clinton

Women played an important role in American national politics even before they obtained the right to vote in 1920. In 1916, Jeannette Rankin of Montana became the first woman elected to the U.S. Congress. In 1925, Nellie Tayloe Ross became the first woman to serve as governor of a state, in Wyoming, which in 1869 had been the first state to grant women the right to vote. In 1933, Franklin Delano Roosevelt (1933–1945) appointed Frances Perkins secretary of labor, making her the first female cabinet member. In 1997, Madeline Albright became the first female secretary of state, the most senior member of the presidential cabinet.

Ten years later, in 2007, Representative Nancy Pelosi of California became the first woman Speaker of the House of Representatives, the third-highest ranking position in American government. In 2008, former First Lady Hillary Clinton ran as a Democratic candidate for president of the United States. Though she lost the presidential primary, the fact that she was a serious contender for the race was an important victory for women. That summer, Clinton delivered a speech at the Democratic National Convention on August 26, 2008, exactly 88 years after American women were granted the right to vote by the passage of the Nineteenth Amendment to the Constitution. Clinton spoke of how far women had come in those 88 years: "My mother was born before women could vote. My daughter got to vote for her mother for president." Later, President Barack Obama (2009-) appointed Clinton to the position of secretary of state.

S

mine, the message I have come to bring to you. I regard the concurrence of the Senate in the constitutional amendment proposing the extension of the suffrage to women as vitally essential to the successful prosecution of the great war of humanity in which we are engaged. . . . It is my duty to win the war and to ask you to remove every obstacle that stands in the way of winning it. . . .

The women of America are too noble and too intelligent and too devoted to be slackers whether you give or withhold this thing that is mere justice; but I know the magic it will work in their thoughts and spirits if you give it them. . . . The tasks of the women lie at the very heart of the war, and I know how much stronger that heart will beat if you do this just thing and show our women that you trust them as much as you in fact and of necessity depend upon them.

Although 17 states had already granted women the right to vote by the time of the passage of the Nineteenth Amendment, it was not until 1920 that the suffragists had finally succeeding in gaining the right for all American women to vote.

See also: Anthony, Susan B.; Nineteenth Amendment; Stanton, Elizabeth Cady.

Further Reading

Adams, Katherine H., and Michael L. Keene. *Alice Paul and the American Suffrage Campaign.* Champaign: University of Illinois Press, 2007.

Baker, Jean A. *Sisters: The Lives of American Suffragists.* New York: Hill & Wang, 2006.

Loos, Pamela. *Elizabeth Cady Stanton.* New York: Chelsea House, 2001.

Rossi, Anne. *Created Equal: Women Campaign for the Right to Vote 1840–1920.* Washington, D.C.: National Geographic Children's Books, 2005.

Steffens, Lincoln (1866–1936)

American investigative journalist and a leader of the so-called **muckrakers**. In the pre–World War I United States, muckrakers were journalists dedicated to exposing corruption and the oppression of big business.

Steffens was born in San Francisco, California, on April 6, 1866, to Joseph Steffens, a prominent middle-class businessman, and Elizabeth Louisa Symes. In 1870, the family moved to Sacramento, the state capital. Joseph Steffens became vice president of the California National Bank and president of the Board of Trade.

Lincoln, called "Lennie" by his family, developed a spiritual crisis at an early age. He was convinced that he could not love. This drove him to spend hours at church, praying for his soul. For a while, he thought he was going to be a preacher.

School, Turmoil, and Change

Steffens left home to attend the University of California, from which he graduated in 1889. Following this, he attended a military school, where his only consolation for the constant boredom was found in terrorizing the younger cadets and breaking the school's many rules. When he was caught smuggling beer onto campus, he was sentenced to 22 days in the guardhouse. Here, Steffens came to the realization that the military life and the decadence he had been involved with were not the life he wanted. Indeed, the only areas in which he excelled while at the school were literature and writing.

His newly discovered passion for academics could not save his educational career. The University of Berkeley would not have him. Steffens's father had to hire a private tutor to teach his son further, and Steffens took the next few years to develop the life he truly wanted. His parents gave him a room and the freedom to come and go as he pleased. He developed a taste for culture and exploration. Eventually, Steffens was accepted as a regular student at Berkeley. By the time he graduated, he had come to resent everything the institution and his father stood for. He believed that the accumulation of wealth was morally bankrupt. And that the discipline required by schools was a prison for the mind. Steffens saw himself as a critic of society.

Because of his disenchantment with American universities, Steffens decided to go to Germany, to attend another institution of higher learning. In Germany, Steffens learned how desperate things were in the United States. By comparison to Berlin, Sacramento was dirty, disorderly, and dangerous. Steffens came to see how American cities were a failure.

CAREER

These experiences prepared Steffens for his career as a critical journalist. At age 26, when he returned from Europe, Steffens received a letter from his father essentially telling him that his days of schooling were over. He was no longer going to receive an allowance from his father and was going to have to earn a living for himself. His father suggested that he stay in New York and learn to make his way.

Making use of his talents as a writer, Steffens got a job working for the *New York Post*. The newspaper demanded that all writing be factually accurate. The editor did not want to publish literature as news. The *Post* had a mission: to root out corruption. While the paper was good at revolting against a broken government, its dispassionate reporting did nothing to help develop a spirit of reform. This was where Steffens broke with the vision of the *Post*'s editor.

In 1901, Steffens became managing editor of *McClure's Magazine*. Along with Ida Tarbell and Ray Stannard Baker, Steffens began writing about government corruption. In 1902, he published an article titled "Tweed Days in St. Louis," one of the first muckraking articles. In 1904, six of Steffens's articles on political corruption were published together as *Shame of Cities*. The articles covered corruption in Chicago, Minneapolis, Pittsburgh, St. Louis, Philadelphia, and New York. The articles and book were a success. Where logical argument may have failed to sway public opinion, Steffens instead appealed to American's pride and emotions. He made them feel ashamed of the state of their country, which prompted them to call for **reform**. Others soon joined in, writing articles and novels to support the muckrakers' crusade.

Steffens eventually fell out of favor in the United States when he began supporting the 1917 **communist** revolution in Russia. His enthusiasm for **communism** made him an outsider, although that enthusiasm eventually died as well. He returned to California and died in 1936.

See also: *McClure's Magazine*; Muckrakers; Tarbell, Ida.

Further Reading

Kaplan, Justin. *Lincoln Steffens.* New York: Simon & Schuster, 2004.

T–W

Taft, William Howard (1857–1930)

Twenty-seventh president of the United States and the only man to be both president and chief justice of the United States. Although he supported progressive reforms, William H. Taft was more **conservative** and did not implement changes as aggressively as other reformers had hoped.

Taft was born on September 15, 1857, in Cincinnati, Ohio, to a powerful political family. His father was Ulysses S. Grant's (1869–1877) secretary of war.

EARLY LIFE

Taft was well educated. In 1874, he attended Yale College and graduated second in his class. To complete his education, Taft attended the Cincinnati Law School. In 1880, he graduated from law school and passed the bar exam.

In 1881, Taft became assistant **prosecutor** for Hamilton County, Ohio. It was an impressive appointment, as he had only passed the bar a few months before. From 1883 to 1887, Taft ran a private law practice. During that time, he married Helen Herron, a sweetheart from his youth.

HIGH–PROFILE JUDICIAL CAREER

Taft was appointed to the Ohio Supreme Court in 1887. Three years later, in 1890, President Benjamin Harrison (1889–1893) made Taft solicitor general of the United States. When a case appears before the Supreme Court, the solicitor general represents the government.

In 1892, Taft was made a judge in the Sixth Circuit Court of Appeals. His decisions were often antilabor. Despite often finding in favor of businesses, Taft also upheld the right of workers to organize.

In 1900, Taft left his position to become chairman of the Second Philippine Commission. The United States had acquired the Philippines, a chain of islands off the southeast coast of Asia, from Spain following the Spanish-American War (1898), and the commission was charged with organizing a civilian government for the new territory. Taft became governor of the Philippines and focused his efforts on developing the economic strength of the islands. Then President Theodore Roosevelt (1901–1909) tried twice to get him to accept an appointment to the U.S. Supreme Court. In 1904, the president convinced him to return to the United States. Taft agreed to be Roosevelt's secretary of war if he could continue to oversee Philippine affairs.

PRESIDENCY

Taft and Roosevelt became good friends, and when Roosevelt decided against running again for president in 1908, he gave Taft his support. Taft was elected president in 1908, defeating Democrat William Jennings Bryan. As Roosevelt's successor, the president's **progressive** supporters expected Taft to continue the same agenda. Progressives, however, were disappointed.

Roosevelt had been an inspiring leader, rallying the public and leading them in the charge against **corruption**. He sought to fix what was wrong with American society, and his enthusiasm and charisma garnered him significant support. Taft did not share Roosevelt's leadership abilities.

Further, Taft did not appoint many progressive Republicans to his cabinet. He also supported the Payne-Aldrich Tariff, which did not significantly lower **tariff** rates. Progressives supported lower tariffs and had expected the president to veto the bill. When he signed it into law, the Republican Party began to suffer internal disagreement. The party became bitterly divided, and Taft could not bring both sides to compromise, much less agreement.

Taft did follow some progressive principles, though. He filed more trust-busting actions than President Roosevelt had. He changed regulations for government workers, bringing about an eight-hour workday. He also passed a bill requiring disclosure of campaign spending, to make elections more transparent.

Taft's final break with the progressive Republicans came when he fired Gifford Pinchot, head of the Bureau of Forestry. Pinchot had been one of Roosevelt's close associates. No one knows exactly when Roosevelt ceased seeing himself as Taft's friend, but by the time Roosevelt returned from an African hunting vacation in 1910, it was clear that they were on different sides. Urged by Progressives who were dissatisfied by Taft's administration, Roosevelt decided to run for president in 1912. The Republican Party split when Roosevelt failed to get the nomination. With popular support split between Taft and Roosevelt, the Democratic candidate, Woodrow Wilson, won the election. Taft won only two states and eight electoral votes, the most crushing defeat suffered by any **incumbent** president.

CHIEF JUSTICE

Taft continued to work in the public sector. In 1921, President Warren G. Harding (1921–1923) appointed him chief justice of the United States. Taft instituted reforms in the Court to improve its efficiency and helped pass the Judge's Act of 1925 to allow the Court more control in choosing its cases.

Taft resigned his post as chief justice in February 1930. He died on March 8, 1930, of heart disease. Taft is the only person to have served as both president and chief justice. Throughout his long career as a public servant, Taft thoughtfully brought about changes to government and society.

See also: Election of 1912; Payne-Aldrich Tariff Act; Roosevelt, Theodore; Wilson, Woodrow.

Further Reading

Anderson, Judith Icke. *William Howard Taft: An Intimate History*. New York: W.W. Norton & Company, 1981.

Benson, Michael. *William Howard Taft*. Minneapolis, Minn.: Lerner Publications, 2007.

Tarbell, Ida (1857–1944)

First great woman journalist, known for exposing business corruption. Commonly referred to as a **muckraker**, Tarbell pioneered investigative journalism and helped bring down the Standard Oil Company. She was born on November 5, 1857, in Hatch Hollow, Pennsylvania. Her parents were both teachers, though they dreamed of the possibilities that life on the frontier offered. After her birth, her father bought a farm in Iowa, but the Panic of 1857 that rocked the banking industry caused the bank to foreclose on the farm before the Tarbells could move.

Ida's father, Franklin, returned to Pennsylvania in 1859. That year, a drilling company struck oil near Titusville, Pennsylvania. In 1860, Franklin moved the family to the oil-rich area and began drilling for oil on his own. Tarbell's childhood was spent among oil derricks and prospectors. She later wrote that it was the women who tried to make Rouseville a real town, with churches and schools. The women fought to keep out the negative influences of saloons and gambling houses.

The family moved to Titusville in time for Ida to enter high school. She graduated in 1875. For a woman of her time, there were few options for the future. Women either got married or worked. Ida Tarbell chose work and supported the women's rights movement that called for extending the right to an education and the right to make a living to women.

In 1876, Tarbell entered Allegheny College, the only woman in her class of 40. After graduating in 1880, she took a job as a teacher in Poland, Ohio. However, the position did not allow her to pursue her interest in science as she had hoped, and after two years, she returned home.

A NEW CAREER

Tarbell's return led to a chance meeting with Dr. Theodore Flood, editor of *The Chautauquan* magazine. He hired Tarbell as an assistant, and she was introduced to her future career. In 1890, she left her position at the magazine to travel to Paris. She wanted to write a well-researched biography on Madame Roland, a figure of the French Revolution. She wrote articles on French life for American magazines in order to support her studies. This freelance writing put her into contact with Samuel McClure.

When Tarbell returned to the United States, McClure offered her a position as an editor at his magazine. She was assigned a biography on President Abraham Lincoln (1861–1865) and began to see how the story of Lincoln and the story of America were part of her personal story as well. The country's problems were hers.

ATTACKING STANDARD OIL

Tarbell's next assignment was the result of talks she had with John Phillips, McClure's business partner, concerning the Standard Oil Company and its effect on her own life. She presented McClure with an idea for another biography, that of Standard Oil. McClure consented, and Tarbell's research began.

Her reports were published as *The History of Standard Oil* in *McClure's Magazine* in 19 parts, starting in 1902. What she had intended as a historical document was labeled muckraking by President Theodore Roosevelt (1901–1909). Tarbell had personally interviewed Henry H. Rogers, chairman of Standard Oil's operating committee. He was candid in his answers, and Tarbell was able to document the company's impressive practices for building an impenetrable monopoly. She revealed that Standard Oil routinely squashed competition through ruthless tactics.

Because of her articles, public opinion was swayed against Standard Oil. The company became the target of an **antitrust** suit by the government. In 1911, the Supreme Court ordered that Standard Oil be broken up and reorganized into 38 companies.

Tarbell left *McClure's* in 1906. She became editor and co-owner of *American Magazine*, where she worked for the next nine years. Following that, Tarbell became a lecturer and took part in public life. Her autobiography, *All in a Day's Work*, was published in 1939. Tarbell died in 1944 at the age of 87.

See also: Muckrakers; *McClure's Magazine*; Steffens, Lincoln.

FURTHER READING

Bausum, Ann. *Muckrakers: How Ida Tarbell, Upton Sinclair, and Lincoln Steffens Helped Expose Scandal, Inspire Reform, and Invent Investigative Journalism.* Des Moines, Iowa: National Geographic Children's Books, 2007.

Weinberg, Steve. *Taking on the Trust: The Epic Battle of Ida Tarbell and John D. Rockefeller.* New York: W.W. Norton & Company, 2008.

Temperance Movement

An organized effort in the nineteenth and early twentieth centuries to encourage people to moderate or stop consuming alcoholic beverages. The temperance movement achieved its goals in 1919 with the passage of the Eighteenth Amendment to the U.S. Constitution.

The Eighteenth Amendment made Prohibition, or the banning of the sale, manufacture, and transportation of alcohol for consumption in the United States, legal. However, in 1933, the Twenty-first Amendment repealed the Eighteenth Amendment, bringing Prohibition to an end.

AN INCREASE IN ALCOHOL USE

During the early nineteenth century, the consumption of alcohol in the United States greatly increased. At the same time, a powerful religious movement swept through the country, denouncing alcohol use as a sin. Many Christian preachers blamed most problems in American society on the consumption of alcohol, including poor health, unemployment, and crime. Local groups formed to promote temperate, or moderate, use of alcohol. In 1826, a national organization, the American Temperance Society, was founded in Boston. It published articles and sent speakers around the country to lecture about the negative effects of alcohol. Within 10 years, it had more than one million members and hundreds of local offices.

By the 1840s, the temperance movement had changed its focus. Now many leaders believed that moderate consumption was no longer enough to improve the ills of American society and believed instead that it was necessary to ban all alcohol. In 1846, Maine became the first state to enact a law prohibiting the sale of alcoholic beverages. By 1855, 12 states had followed Maine's example and passed prohibition laws of their own. Yet the laws were difficult to enforce, and many people did not support them. By 1868, Maine was the only state left with a liquor prohibition law, and the temperance movement appeared to have lost the fight against alcohol.

However, as the Progressive movement began to take shape in the late 1800s, its leaders revived the temperance movement. The **Progressives** sought to reform nearly all social and political aspects of American society. They felt that banning the consumption of alcohol would solve many of the worst problems in society, including poverty and crime. Some Progressives were convinced that the millions of new **immigrants** arriving from southern and eastern Europe during the late 1800s drank too much and thought that Prohibition would help turn these immigrants into reformed American citizens.

WOMEN AND THE TEMPERANCE MOVEMENT

Because many women had firsthand experiences of the negative effects of liquor on families, they were strong supporters of a complete ban on alcohol. In addition, many leaders in the temperance movement were women. At the time, many social reformers took the view that women were morally superior to men. Therefore, they believed that women should be leaders of a movement that aimed to protect family life. According to women's rights leader Catherine A. Hoffman, ". . . the men would not do it, [so] we women did it. . . . This conduct from us women means something."

The temperance movement also appealed to many women because it allowed them a political voice at a time when they could not vote in national elections. Politicians in the 1800s cited drunkenness at the polls as one reason for denying women the vote, which induced some women to support a ban on alcoholic beverages. Many women involved in the temperance movement were also women's rights activists, as the movements were closely related. Notable leaders in both movements included Susan B. Anthony, Frances E. Willard, and Carry Nation.

The Women's Temperance Union The Women's Christian Temperance Union, founded in 1874, was at the time the largest women's organization in the country. Members of the groups spoke publicly in favor of prohibition and lobbied elected officials for laws banning the consumption of alcohol. Liquor stores and saloons, where men came to drink, were often sites of gambling, prostitution, and other illegal activities. For this reason, they were popular targets of prohibitionists. Some of the more active members disrupted these businesses.

Carry Nation became a well-known temperance activist who took matters into her own hands when Kansas authorities were unable to enforce prohibition laws. Nation had been briefly married to an alcoholic in the late 1800s and supported complete prohibition. Starting in 1900, in Kiowa, Kansas, she became known for bursting into saloons with a hatchet, smashing liquor bottles and breaking furniture. Between 1900 and 1910, she was arrested at least 30 times after leading groups of women into various saloons. Nation believed she was doing God's will by destroying saloons. She claimed that a voice had told her, "Take something in your hands, and throw at these places in Kiowa and smash them." Nation's notorious raids on saloons made her a vivid symbol of the temperance movement.

The Anti–Saloon League In addition to the Women's Christian Temperance Union, the Anti-Saloon League of America was another important and powerful temperance organization in the United States. In 1893, temperance supporters in Oberlin, Ohio, had formed the Ohio Anti-Saloon League with the goal of reducing, or possibly prohibiting, alcohol consumption by enforcing prohibition laws and trying to establish new ones. In the same year, temperance supporters in Washington, D.C., formed their own Anti-Saloon League. In 1895, both groups united to create the National Anti-Saloon League, which eventually became the Anti-Saloon League of America.

Like the Women's Christian Temperance Union, the Anti-Saloon League focused on implementing antialcohol laws in local communities. The group used local churches to recruit followers to join their cause. As support grew, the League began a campaign to implement Prohibition nationwide. The organization also lobbied members of both major political parties, Democrats and Republicans, to support Prohibition. The league sent hundreds of letters and petitions to the U.S. Congress, demanding the prohibition of alcohol.

In 1913, the Anti-Saloon League sponsored a parade in Washington, D.C. After this parade, they presented an amendment to the U.S. Congress that would be the basis for the Eighteenth Amendment to the Constitution.

When the United States entered World War I (1914–1918) to fight against Germany, Prohibition began to seem patriotic, as many brewers in the United States were German Americans. The Anti-Saloon League convinced many people that to support Prohibition was to support those Americans fighting Germans in the war.

By 1916, 19 states already prohibited the manufacture and sale of alcoholic beverages. Because of increasing pressure from the various organizations of the temperance movement, Congress finally passed the Eighteenth Amendment in December 1917. It became law in January 1919, when 36 of the 48 states in the Union had **ratified** it. Later that year, the Volstead Act, which enforced Prohibition by stating that "no person shall manufacture, sell, barter, transport, import, export, deliver, or furnish any intoxicating liquor except as authorized by this act" was passed. Prohibition officially went into effect in January 1920.

PROHIBITION FAILS

Many Americans remained divided by Prohibition. After 14 years, it was ultimately declared a failure because it had simply made the buying and selling of alcohol a prosperous, though illegal, business. In February 1933, a resolution proposing a

Twenty-first Amendment to repeal the Eighteenth Amendment was introduced into Congress. In December of that year, the Twenty-first Amendment was ratified by the necessary two-thirds majority of the states.

See also: Eighteenth Amendment; Prohibition; Twenty-first Amendment.

Further Reading

Gifford, Catolyn De Swarte, and Amy R. Slagell, eds. *Let Something Good Be Said: Speeches and Writings of Frances E. Willard.* Champaign: University of Illinois Press, 2007.

Grace, Fran. *Carry A. Nation: Retelling the Life.* Bloomington: Indiana University Press, 2008.

Lieurance, Suzanne. *The Prohibition Era in American History.* Berkeley Heights, N.J.: Enslow Publishers, 2003.

Lucas, Eileen. *The Eighteenth and Twenty-First Amendments: Alcohol—Prohibition and Repeal.* Berkeley Heights, N.J.: Enslow Publishers, 1998.

Twenty-first Amendment (1933)

Amendment to the U.S. Constitution, **ratified** in 1933, which repealed the Eighteenth Amendment, thereby ending Prohibition. By the early 1930s, it was clear that the nation's attempt to prevent the sale, manufacture, and consumption or use of intoxicating beverages, as required by the Eighteenth Amendment, was not successful.

The restrictions on alcohol had led to bootlegging, the illegal manufacture and sale of such beverages. It also had led to the opening of speakeasies, secret bars and clubs where the illegally acquired alcohol was served. Furthermore, all these activities caused a sharp increase in **organized crime**, as mobsters competed to make money selling and supplying the illegal alcohol.

During the presidential election of 1932, the Democratic Party called for the end of Prohibition. After Franklin D. Roosevelt (1933–1945) won a sweeping electoral victory, he called on Congress to repeal the Eighteenth Amendment. In response, the Congress proposed the Twenty-first Amendment on February 20, 1933.

However, many people feared that if the proposed amendment was submitted to the state legislatures it might not be ratified by the needed three-fourths of the states. This belief was based on the fact that many state legislatures were from districts controlled by rural voters. Because rural voters were against alcohol consumption and thereby tended to favor Prohibition, their legislators would likely vote against the proposed amendment and block its approval.

Therefore, Congress called for special state conventions to ratify the amendment. The delegates to these conventions were to be elected by the voters of the entire state, not by legislative districts. Thus, the delegates would likely be more apt to reflect the view of urban, or city, voters, people who generally favored the end of Prohibition.

The proposed amendment was ratified on December 5, 1933. It is the only amendment thus far ratified by state conventions, specially

History Speaks

Overturning Prohibition

Ratified in 1933, The Twenty-first Amendment to the U.S. Constitution repealed the Eighteenth Amendment. Passed in 1919, the Eighteenth Amendment initiated the era of Prohibition—a time when the manufacture, sale, and consumption of alcoholic beverages were outlawed in the United States and its territories. After 14 years of Prohibition, it became clear that this attempt at social **reform** was not successful.

Section 1. The eighteenth article of amendment to the Constitution of the United States is hereby repealed.

Section 2. The transportation or importation into any State, Territory, or possession of the United States for delivery or use therein of intoxicating liquors, in violation of the laws thereof, is hereby prohibited.

Section 3. This article shall be inoperative unless it shall have been ratified as an amendment to the Constitution by conventions in the several States, as provided in the Constitution, within seven years from the date of the submission hereof to the States by the Congress.

selected for the purpose; all other amendments to the U.S. Constitution have been ratified by state legislatures. It is also the only amendment that was passed for the explicit purpose of repealing an earlier amendment to the Constitution.

See also: Eighteenth Amendment; Prohibition; Temperance Movement.

Further Reading

Kahn, Gordon, and Al Hirschfield. *The Speakeasies of 1932.* Milwaukee, Wis.: Glenn Young/Applause Books, 2005.

Lieurance, Suzanne. *The Prohibition Era in American History.* Berkeley Heights, N.J.: Enslow Publishers, 2003.

Lucas, Elizabeth. *The Eighteenth and Twenty-First Amendments: Alcohol—Prohibition and Repeal.* Berkeley Heights, N.J.: Enslow Publishers, 1998.

Veblen, Thorstein (1857–1929)

Economist, social thinker, and author of the important work *The Theory of the Leisure Class* (1899). In this book, Veblen argued that people in society chase after **social status** by acquiring wealth.

Veblen was born on July 30, 1857, in Cato, Wisconsin, to hardworking **immigrant** parents. His parents valued education, and he began school at age five. In 1880, Veblen graduated from Carleton College with a degree in economics. He attended graduate school at Johns Hopkins University and got his doctorate in 1884 from Yale.

Veblen's ideas were greatly influenced by the biologist Charles Darwin and the philosopher Herbert Spencer, two influential men of the mid-1800s. Spencer had taken Darwin's understanding of **evolution** and applied it to all aspects of life, not just biological change and development over a long period of time. Human societies, he proposed, underwent a process of evolution, or change, of their own. Spencer coined the phrase "survival of the fittest." He believed that this theory should rule humanity's actions. Veblen transferred the idea of "survival of the fittest" into an economic concept.

THE THEORY OF THE LEISURE CLASS

In 1899, Veblen published *The Theory of the Leisure Class.* It was Veblen's first major work and his most influential book. Earlier economic theory had suggested that all human beings craved pleasure. All human actions, therefore, were a direct result of seeking pleasure and avoiding pain. This theory, however, did not give humans any motivation of their own. It contended that humans simply responded to their surroundings. Veblen found this idea to be overly simple.

Instead, he believed that humans were evolving and changing beings. They developed habits that affected their actions as they sought better economic circumstances. Their societies, for example, developed economies and institutions based on their surroundings and the challenges they encountered.

After Veblen applied his analysis to modern industrial economies, he was seen as a social thinker. He believed that modern economies broke people into two groups: those who made goods and those who made money. These two groups were in constant opposition. Most economists of the time saw men of wealth as the ultimate expression of "survival of the fittest." Veblen, however, took a radically different view. He accused those who made money as being parasites, feeding off the work and innovation of those who made goods.

CONSPICUOUS CONSUMPTION

In addition, Veblen analyzed the forces of competition in society. His insights are still felt today. Veblen coined the term *conspicuous consumption*. According to his theory, humans competed with one another for recognition and esteem by gaining wealth and vast quantities of goods by spending huge amounts of money. By displaying one's wealth through conspicuous consumption, according to Veblen, people earned the envy and esteem of others. This process was endless. So conspicuous consumption led to conspicuous and ongoing waste, which Veblen found morally irresponsible.

The leisure class, in particular, used conspicuous consumption to both cement their place in society and compete with one another. Because they did not have to work, they invested their time in competitive games, which acted as a substitute for real competition for goods, food, and housing.

In the late 1800s, as the middle-class grew, more people began to strive for surplus wealth and goods and felt themselves failures if they did not achieve it. Veblen noted that the poor in the modern era, who were basically better cared for, fed, and housed than the poor of 100 years earlier, felt more wretched than their forebears. Their sense of failure was much greater because the surrounding culture promoted the idea that everyone should be able to consume in excess.

Modern advertising techniques still heavily depend on the idea that everyone wants to outdo his or her neighbor and will be willing to buy a product to prove it. While Veblen wrote a number of other books expanding upon *The Theory of the Leisure Class*, none reached the same level of success. Veblen's major work, however, not only influenced progressive reforms of his time, it continues to be an important socioeconomic study today.

See also: Social Darwinism.

Further Reading

Patsouras, Louis. *Thorstein Veblen and the American Way of Life*. Tonawanda, N.Y.: Black Rose Press, 2004.

Wells-Barnett, Ida B. (1862–1931)

African American journalist and civil rights activist who led a crusade against **lynching**. Wells was also a **muckraker** and social reformer who supported and fought for progressive **reforms** during her career.

EARLY LIFE

Ida B. Wells was born to enslaved parents on July 16, 1862, in Holly Springs, Mississippi. With the end of the Civil War (1861–1865), Wells's family became free. Her father, Jim Wells, was politically active. He was a member of a local black political organization and campaigned for black candidates.

As a young child, Wells went to Shaw University, a school in Holly Springs for blacks. Very few blacks could read, and Wells's parents considered learning to read of great importance. Her parents died in 1878 of yellow fever. To keep her family together following the death of her parents, Wells became a teacher at age 16. In 1884, she moved to Memphis, Tennessee, so she could go to Fisk University during the summer. During the rest of the year, she taught first grade.

While in Tennessee, Wells filed a law suit against the Chesapeake & Ohio Railroad for forcing her to move to a "colored" car. Her suit went to the Tennessee Supreme Court in 1887, but the courts found against her. Incensed by the injustice she had suffered, Wells started to become politically active. In addition to teaching and studying, she began writing articles for newspapers. In 1891, an article complaining that the Memphis School Board underfunded black schools cost her her teaching job.

CAREER IN JOURNALISM

After that incident, Wells invested herself fulltime in journalism. She became part owner of the *Memphis Free Speech* newspaper. In 1892, three of Wells's friends, businessmen, were lynched. In response, she began writing anti-lynching editorials. Her newspaper's offices were attacked and sacked by a white mob. Her printing press was destroyed. Wells was in Philadelphia at the time and therefore escaped a lynching herself.

Following the attack, Wells moved to New York City and wrote for *The New York Age*, an African American newspaper. She continued her campaign against lynching, which had grown disastrously common in the post-war South. In 1893, Wells began a lecture tour in Great Britain. In 1894, she met and married Ferdinand Barnett, owner of the *Conservator*, the first black newspaper in Chicago.

In 1901, Wells published *Lynching and the Excuse for It*. Her thesis was that the aim of lynching was not simply the killing of another black, but discouraging political involvement from all blacks in the South. This would ensure that whites maintained complete control. In a 1909 speech, Wells noted:

> Proof that lynching follows the color line is to be found in the statistics, which have been kept for the past twenty-five years. During the few years preceding this period and while frontier law existed, the executions showed a majority of white victims. Later, however, as law courts and authorized judiciary extended into the far West, lynch law rapidly abated, and its white victims became few and far between.
>
> During the last ten years, from 1899 to 1908 inclusive, the number lynched was 959. Of this number, 102 were white, while the colored victims numbered 857. No other nation, civilized or savage, burns its criminals; only under that Stars and Stripes is the human holocaust possible. Twenty-eight human beings burned at the stake, one of them a woman and two of them children, is the awful indictment against American civilization—the gruesome tribute which the nation pays to the color line.
>
> Why is mob murder permitted by a Christian nation? What is the cause of this awful slaughter? This question is answered almost daily: always the same shameless falsehood that "Negroes are lynched to protect womanhood." Standing before a Chautauqua assemblage, John Temple Graves, at once champion of lynching and apologist for lynchers, said, "The mob stands today as the most potential bulwark between the women of the South and such a carnival of crime as would infuriate the world and precipitate the annihilation of the Negro race." This is the never-varying answer of lynchers and their apologists. All know that it is untrue. The cowardly lyncher revels in murder, then seeks to shield himself from public execration by claiming devotion to woman. But truth is mighty and the lynching record discloses

the hypocrisy of the lyncher as well as his crime.

In addition to her anti-lynching work, Wells also worked for women's rights. In particular, she supported women's suffrage and organized Chicago's Alpha Suffrage Club, a black woman suffrage organization. She also organized the National Association of Colored Women.

Although Wells is often credited with helping to found the National Association for the Advancement of Colored People (NAACP), she was not involved with the organization beyond attending the conference where it was founded. She did, however, convince the NAACP to pursue the outlawing of lynching at the federal level. In general, though, Wells was more radical than the NAACP. She believed that blacks should achieve equality through their own efforts and should not depend on supportive whites.

Ida Wells died on March 25, 1931, of uremia, an illness caused by kidney failure. Her autobiography was not published until 1970.

See also: Social Justice.

Further Reading

Giddings, Paula J. *Ida: A Sword Among Lions: Ida B. Wells and the Campaign Against Lynching*. New York: Amistad Press, 2008.

Wilson, Woodrow (1856–1924)

Twenty-eighth president of the United States and leader who saw the country through World War I (1914–1918). Woodrow Wilson (1913–1921), an idealist, helped to found the League of Nations, even though he could not get his own country to join it. Wilson was also a **progressive** president who worked for **reform** within the United States.

EARLY LIFE

Wilson was born on December 28, 1856, in Staunton, Virginia. Because his father was a Presbyterian minister, the family moved quite often as his father moved to different churches to preach. The Wilsons were in Augusta, Georgia, during the Civil War (1861–1865), and Wilson's father's church was made into a hospital. As a young boy, Woodrow witnessed the horrors of war, which had a lasting effect on him.

Wilson had difficulty as a student. Some historians attribute his inability to read until he was 11 to dyslexia, a learning disability that hampers reading and spelling. Others point to the poor state of education in the South during Reconstruction (1865–1877). At any rate, he did not start school until he was nine and could not read until two years later. He was always a slow reader, despite developing an interest in literature.

Wilson briefly attended Davidson College in North Carolina before being accepted to what is now Princeton University in 1875. While at Princeton, Wilson became editor of the school paper. He read avidly and led an active and successful academic life. One of his most noted accomplishments was an essay he wrote comparing the American form of government to the British Parliament. He graduated from Princeton in 1879 and went on to study law at the University of Virginia.

In 1882, Wilson received his law degree and passed the bar exam. He spent two years practicing law but found the profession unfulfilling. Instead, he went back to school, enrolling as a graduate student at Johns Hopkins University. In 1886, he earned a Ph.D. in history and political science—the only American president to have this advanced degree.

MOVE TO PRINCETON UNIVERSITY

Wilson taught at Bryn Mawr and Wesleyan colleges before attaining a position at Princeton University. His teaching career flourished. Wilson became the highest paid professor on staff and president of the university in 1902. Wilson worked to reform the university's structure and change the curriculum. He wished to transform Princeton into an ideal college of higher learning, with core disciplines and rigorous academic departments. He also wished to change the university's social structure from one based on elite clubs for wealthy gentlemen to a more homogenized blending of graduates and undergrads undertaking serious studies. Many of Wilson's attempted reforms met with failure, as Princeton alumni fiercely opposed changes.

GOVERNOR OF NEW JERSEY

In 1910, Wilson left Princeton to run for governor of New Jersey as a member of the Democratic Party. After winning the election, Wilson implemented a number of progressive changes. He instituted campaign finance reform and fought against the party boss system by instituting **primary elections.** Wilson also introduced **workers' compensation** in New Jersey. These reforms gave Wilson substantial ground on which to run for national office.

REFORM PRESIDENT

In 1912, Wilson ran for president against former president Theodore Roosevelt (1901–1909), who was running as a candidate of the newly created Progressive Party, and **incumbent** Republican president William Howard Taft (1909–1913). Because the Republican voters were split between Roosevelt and Taft, Wilson won the election. His plan for the country was called "New Freedom," and despite being from the opposite party of the previous two presidents, he continued their progressive reform agenda.

New Freedom The New Freedom called for lower tariffs, a progressive Republican stance that Taft had abandoned, laws curtailing abusive business practices by large corporations, and banking reform. Wilson's skill as a speaker helped push these reforms through. Unlike presidents before him, Wilson conducted himself like a British prime minister. He appeared personally before Congress to secure support for a legislative agenda that he had prepared before entering the White House.

To ensure that his reforms were passed, Wilson also kept Congress in session for nearly a year and a half. This was unprecedented, but his strategy worked. Among the legislation Wilson supported was the Underwood-Simmons Tariff, lowering

HISTORY MAKERS

Thomas R. Marshall (1854–1925)

Thomas Marshall, a progressive Republican lawyer and governor, went on to serve two terms as vice president under Woodrow Wilson (1913–1921). Marshall was born on March 14, 1854, in North Manchester, Indiana. As a young boy, he often spent his spare time at the courthouse in order to listen to the lawyers there present their cases.

After earning his bachelor's degree in 1873, Marshall began to study law under Judge Walter Olds. On his 21st birthday, he passed the bar exam and opened up a practice in Columbia City. The Democratic Party nominated him for the position of **prosecutor**, but he was running in a heavily Republican district and lost.

Marshall had a reputation as an articulate and persuasive speaker. This ability gained him the Democratic nomination for governor in 1908. He won the election and began a program of social reform in Indiana. **Child labor laws** were passed, as well as legislation on employer liability to help protect workers.

Based on his record in Indiana, the Democratic Party decided to nominate Marshall as the vice-presidential candidate in the 1912 election. He became Woodrow Wilson's running mate, even though Wilson was not particularly impressed with him. For his part, Marshall was initially uninterested in the vice presidency. He turned down the nomination at first, until his wife convinced him to run. Marshall had little experience for the position. He was not a legislator or business leader. He only had four years in any administrative capacity and had no military experience. Despite these shortcomings, he was a surprisingly effective vice president.

Marshall's greatest influence was his ability to sway legislators. He was quick-witted and good-humored, which gained him many friends. Marshall supported strict neutrality in World War I (1914–1918), a stance that he later came to regret. He also supported the League of Nations, although the United States never became a member.

When Wilson suffered a stroke that prevented him from governing the nation, Marshall refused to take over the office—even as acting president—without written requests from Wilson's wife, doctor, and an accompanying congressional resolution. This situation left the country adrift. As a result, Edith Wilson prevented anyone except the president's doctors from seeing him. She screened all mail and brought important papers and legislation to the bedridden president. While Marshall was considered as a possible candidate in the next presidential election, he did not seek the nomination. Marshall died on June 1, 1925, in Washington, D.C.

tariffs for the first time in 40 years. He also created the Federal Reserve to give the government more control over the economy. The Clayton Antitrust Act put restrictions on business and strengthened the ability of labor unions to fight for fair working conditions. He also created the Federal Trade Commission (FTC) to oversee businesses.

In addition to these reforms, Wilson also urged Congress to pass legislation that limited railroad workers to eight-hour workdays, abolished child labor, and granted government loans to farmers. Many progressive Republicans were drawn to his side. These reforms are especially notable because the balance of power in Congress had shifted away from the Democrats in 1914.

Foreign Affairs While Wilson's domestic policies were successful, his foreign affairs policies proved less so. World War I began in Europe in 1914. Wilson was an **isolationist** at the time, striving to remain neutral, at least when it came to war in Europe. The United States participated in a number of military actions in Latin America and Mexico. U.S. forces invaded Haiti and the Dominican Republic. In 1916, American troops attempted to hunt down Pancho Villa, a Mexican revolutionary who sent raids across the border into New Mexico.

In 1915, German submarines sank the *Lusitania*, a British liner. One hundred and twenty-eight Americans died, and many in the United States called for war. Instead, Wilson worked to maintain the nation's official neutrality and pursued peace. He asked the Germans to cease their submarine attacks, and the United States was able to stay out of the war throughout 1916.

In 1917, after winning reelection the previous year, Wilson attempted to end World War I by offering to mediate peace. He asked warring nations what their terms for peace would be and pledged to help create a "league of nations" in which grievances could be aired and resolutions reached without the need for war.

His efforts were in vain. The Germans began using their submarines again on February 1. In addition, British intelligence intercepted a telegram from Arthur Zimmermann, the German foreign minister, to the German ambassador in the United States detailing a plan to encourage war between Mexico and the United States. In the face of such provocation, Wilson had no choice but to join the war. Five weeks after the telegram, known as the Zimmermann Note, was made public, the United States Congress declared war on Germany and the **Central powers**.

In his war message to Congress, delivered on April 2, 1917, the president declared:

> . . . The world must be made safe for **democracy**. Its peace must be planted upon the tested foundations of political liberty. We have no selfish ends to serve. We desire no conquest, no dominion. We seek no indemnities for ourselves, no material compensation for the sacrifices we shall freely make. We are but one of

> the champions of the rights of mankind. We shall be satisfied when those rights have been made as secure as the faith and the freedom of nations can make them. . . .

A year and a half after the United States joined World War I, the Germans sued for peace. At the 11th hour on the 11th day of the 11th month of 1918, the war was declared over. Wilson traveled to France to attend the Paris Peace Conference, hoping to secure a just peace and establish the League of Nations. The resulting Treaty of Versailles placed harsh terms on the Central powers, made significant territorial changes in Europe, and imposed financial restitution on the defeated nations. The treaty did, however, establish the League of Nations, which he believed would lead to lasting peace.

The conference had been a great strain on Wilson's health. When he returned to the United States, he found political opposition waiting for him. Senate Republicans rejected the League of Nations and would not ratify the Treaty of Versailles. In an attempt to secure its passage, Wilson toured the country, giving a remarkable number of speeches–39 in 3 weeks. This intense schedule further strained his failing health. On September 25, 1919, he nearly had a nervous breakdown, and on October 2, he suffered a stroke that left him partially paralyzed. The United States never joined the League of Nations, and Wilson never fully recovered from his stroke.

In the presidential election of 1920, Republicans won a sweeping victory. They took the win as proof that the country rejected Wilson's Progressivism and stance in international politics. Wilson died in his home on February 3, 1924, still believing that an international governing body, such as the League of Nations, could prevent future war.

See also: Child Labor; Election of 1912; Social Justice; Roosevelt, Theodore; Taft, William Howard.

Further Reading

Brands, H.W. *Woodrow Wilson*. New York: Times Books, 2003.

Chace, James. *1912: Wilson, Roosevelt, Taft and Debs—The Election That Changed the Country*. New York: Simon & Schuster, 2005.

Lukes, Bonnie L. *Woodrow Wilson and the Progressive Era*. Greensboro, N.C.: Morgan Reynolds Publishing, 2005.

Maynard, W. Barksdale. *Woodrow Wilson*. New Haven, Conn.: Yale University Press, 2008.

Woman Suffrage

See Social Justice, Suffragists.

Viewpoints About Progressivism

Woman Suffrage, Elizabeth Cady Stanton 1868

Women's rights pioneer Elizabeth Cady Stanton (1815–1902) gave this powerful speech in 1868 at the Women's Suffrage Convention in Washington, D.C. Twenty years earlier, at Seneca Falls, New York, she had helped to launch the women's rights movement in America. Stanton worked tirelessly for more than half a century to obtain voting rights for American women and also questioned the social and political norms of her day which excluded women.

"I urge a sixteenth amendment, because "manhood suffrage," or a man's government, is civil, religious, and social disorganization. The male element is a destructive force, stern, selfish, aggrandizing, loving war, violence, conquest, acquisition, breeding in the material and moral world alike discord, disorder, disease, and death. See what a record of blood and cruelty the pages of history reveal! Through what slavery, slaughter, and sacrifice, through what inquisitions and imprisonments, pains and persecutions, black codes and gloomy creeds, the soul of humanity has struggled for the centuries, while mercy has veiled her face and all hearts have been dead alike to love and hope!

The male element has held high carnival thus far; it has fairly run riot from the beginning, overpowering the feminine element everywhere, crushing out all the diviner qualities in human nature, until we know but little of true manhood and womanhood, of the latter comparatively nothing, for it has scarce been recognized as a power until within the last century. Society is but the reflection of man himself, untempered by woman's thought; the hard iron rule we feel alike in the church, the state, and the home. No one need wonder at the disorganization, at the fragmentary condition of everything, when we remember that man, who represents but half a complete being, with but half an idea on every subject, has undertaken the absolute control of all sublunary matters.

People object to the demands of those whom they choose to call the strong-minded, because they say "the right of suffrage will make the women masculine." That is just the difficulty in which we are involved today. Though disfranchised, we have few women in the best sense; we have simply so many reflections, varieties, and dilutions of the masculine gender. The strong, natural characteristics of womanhood are repressed and ignored in dependence, for so long as man feeds woman she will try to please the giver and adapt herself to his condition. To keep a foothold in society, woman must be as near like man as possible, reflect his ideas, opinions, virtues, motives, prejudices, and vices. She must respect his statutes, though they strip her of every inalienable right, and conflict with that higher law written by the finger of God on her own soul.

She must look at everything from its dollar-and-cent point of view, or she is a mere romancer. She must accept things as they are and make the best of them. To mourn over the miseries of others, the poverty of the poor, their hardships in jails, prisons, asylums, the horrors of war, cruelty, and brutality in every form, all this would be mere sentimentalizing. To protest against the intrigue, bribery, and corruption of public life, to desire that her sons might follow some business that did not involve lying, cheating, and a hard, grinding selfishness, would be arrant nonsense.

In this way man has been molding woman to his ideas by direct and positive influences, while she, if not a negation, has used indirect means to control him, and in most cases developed the very characteristics both in him and herself that needed repression. And now man himself stands appalled at the results of his own excesses, and mourns in bitterness that falsehood, selfishness, and violence are the law of life. The need of this hour is not territory, gold mines, railroads, or specie payments but a new evangel of womanhood, to exalt purity, virtue, morality, true religion, to lift man up into the higher realms of thought and action.

We ask woman's enfranchisement, as the first step toward the recognition of that essential element in government that can only secure the health, strength, and prosperity of the nation. Whatever is done to lift woman to her true position will help to usher in a new day of peace and perfection for the race. ”

Speech After Being Convicted for Voting, Susan B. Anthony, 1872

When Susan B. Anthony, a tireless campaigner for women's rights, voted in the 1872 presidential election, she was arrested. In the excerpt below, Anthony justifies her belief that she did not break the law and that women have the same rights as men.

"Friends and fellow citizens: I stand before you tonight under indictment for the alleged crime of having voted at the last presidential election, without having a lawful right to vote. It shall be my work this evening to prove to you that in thus doing, I not only committed no crime, but, instead, simply exercised my citizen's rights, guaranteed to me and all United States citizens by the National Constitution, beyond the power of any State to deny.

Our democratic-republican government is based on the idea of the natural right of every individual member thereof to a voice and a vote in making and executing the laws. We assert the province of government to be to secure the people in the enjoyment of their inalienable right. We throw to the winds the old dogma that government can give rights. No one denies that before governments were organized each individual possessed the right to protect his own life, liberty and property. When 100 to 1,000,000 people enter into a free government, they do not barter away their natural rights; they simply pledge themselves to protect each other in the enjoyment of them through prescribed judicial and legislative tribunals. They agree to abandon the methods of brute force in the adjustment of their differences and adopt those of civilization . . . The Declaration of Independence, the United States Constitution, the constitutions of the several States and the organic laws of the Territories, all alike propose to *protect* the people in the exercise of their God-given rights. Not one of them pretends to bestow rights.

All men are created equal, and endowed by their Creator with certain inalienable rights. Among these are life, liberty and the pursuit of happiness. To secure these, governments are instituted among men, deriving their just powers from the consent of the governed . . .

The preamble of the Federal Constitution says:

We, the people of the United States, in order to form a more perfect union, establish justice, insure domestic tranquility, provide for the common defense, promote the general welfare, and secure the blessings of liberty to ourselves and our posterity, do ordain and establish this Constitution for the United States of America.

It was we, the people; not we, the white male citizens; nor we, the male citizens; but we, the whole people, who formed the Union. And we formed it, not to give the blessings of liberty, but to secure them; not to the half of ourselves and the half of our posterity, but to the whole people—women as well as men. And it is a downright mockery to talk to women of their enjoyment of the blessings of liberty while they are denied the use of the only means of securing them provided by this democratic-republican government—the ballot . . .

Though the words persons, people, inhabitants, electors, citizens, are all used indiscriminately in the national and State constitutions, there was always a conflict of opinion, prior to the war, as to whether they were synonymous terms, but whatever room there was for doubt, under the old regime, the adoption of the Fourteenth amendment settled that question forever in its first sentence:

All persons born or naturalized in the United States, and subject to the jurisdiction thereof, are citizens of the United States, and of the State wherein they reside.

The second settles the equal status of all citizens:

No State shall make or enforce any law which shall abridge the privileges or immunities of citizens of the United States; nor shall any State deprive any person of life, liberty or property without due process of law, or deny to any person within its jurisdiction the equal protection of the laws.

For any state to make sex a qualification that must ever result in the disfranchisement of one entire half of the people, is to pass a bill of attainder, or, an ex post facto law, and is therefore a violation of the supreme law of the land. By it the blessings of liberty are forever withheld from women and their female posterity.

The only question left to be settled now is: Are women persons? I scarcely believe any of our opponents will have the hardihood to say they are not. Being persons, then, women are citizens, and no State has a right to make any new law, or to enforce any old law, which shall abridge their privileges or immunities. Hence, every discrimination against women in the constitutions and laws of the several States is today null and void, precisely as is every one against negroes. ”

From The Theory of the Leisure Class, Thorstein Veblen, 1899

The Norwegian-American economist Thorstein Veblen (1857–1929) published the book *The Theory of the Leisure Class* in 1899, while he was a professor at the University of Chicago. Veblen claimed he wrote the book as a personal essay criticizing contemporary culture, rather than as an economics textbook. Nonetheless, *Theory of the Leisure Class* is considered one of the great works of economics as well as the first detailed critique of consumerism. In this excerpt, he describes how the leisure class, or the wealthy, developed in society.

"As wealth accumulates, the leisure class develops further in function and structure, and there arises a differentiation within the class. There is a more or less elaborate system of rank and grades. This differentiation is furthered by the inheritance of wealth and the consequent inheritance of gentility. With the inheritance of gentility goes the inheritance of obligatory leisure; and gentility of a sufficient potency to entail a life of leisure may be inherited without the complement of wealth required to maintain a dignified leisure. Gentle blood may be transmitted without goods enough to afford a reputably free consumption at one's ease. Hence results a class of impecunious [poor] gentlemen of leisure, incidentally referred to already. These half-caste gentlemen of leisure fall into a system of hierarchical gradations. Those who stand near the higher and the highest grades of the wealthy leisure class, in point of birth, or in point of wealth, or both, outrank the remoter-born and the pecuniarily [monetarily] weaker. These lower grades, especially the impecunious, or marginal, gentlemen of leisure, affiliate themselves by a system of dependence or fealty to the great ones; by so doing they gain an increment of repute, or of the means with which to lead a life of leisure, from their patron. They become his courtiers or retainers, servants; and being fed and countenanced by their patron they are indices of his rank and vicarious consumer of his superfluous wealth. Many of these affiliated gentlemen of leisure are at the same time lesser men of substance in their own right; so that some of them are scarcely at all, others only partially, to be rated as vicarious consumers. So many of them, however, as make up the retainer and hangers-on of the patron may be classed as vicarious consumer without qualification. Many of these again, and also many of the other aristocracy of less degree, have in turn attached to their persons a more or less comprehensive group of vicarious consumer in the persons of their wives and children, their servants, retainers, etc."

From History of the Standard Oil Company, Ida Tarbell, 1904

Ida Tarbell (1857–1944) published *The History of the Standard Oil Company* in 1904. The inspiration for the book came from her father's being bankrupted by the business practices of oil billionaire John D. Rockefeller Sr., the president of Standard Oil.

Tarbell exposed Rockefeller's ruthless tactics and their destructive effect on smaller oil businesses. Her book fueled negative public feelings against Standard Oil and was a contributing factor in the U.S. government's antitrust actions against the Standard Oil Trust. The U.S. Supreme Court ordered the company broken up in 1911. This excerpt describes some of the business practices used by Rockefeller.

"Mr. Rockefeller was certainly now in an excellent condition to work out his plan of bringing under his own control all the refineries of the country. The Standard Oil Company owned in each of the great refining centres. New York, Pittsburg [sic] and Philadelphia, a large and aggressive plant run by the men who had built it up. These works were, so far as the public knew, still independent and their only relation that of the "Central Association." As a matter of fact they were the "Central Association." Not only had Mr. Rockefeller brought these powerful interests into his concern; he had secured for them a rebate of ten per cent, on a rate which should always be as low as any one of the roads gave any of his competitors. He had done away with middlemen, that is, he was "paying nobody a profit." He had undeniably a force wonderfully constructed for what he wanted to do and one made practically Impregnable as things were in the oil business then, by virtue of its special transportation rate.

As soon as his new line was complete the work of acquiring all outside refineries began at each of the oil centres. Unquestionably the acquisitions were made through persuasion when this was possible. If the party approached refused to lease or sell, he was told firmly what Mr. Rockefeller had told the Cleveland refiners when he went to them in 1872 with the South Improvement contracts, that there was no hope for him; that a combination was in progress which was bound to work; and that those who stayed out would inevitably go to the wall. Naturally the first fruits to fall, into the hands of the new alliance were those refineries which were embarrassed or

(continues)

(continued)

discouraged by the conditions which Mr. Rogers explains above. Take as an example the case of the Citizens' Oil Refining Company of Pittsburg [sic], as it was explained in 1888 to the House Committee on Manufactures in its trust investigation. A. H. Tack, a partner in the company, told the story:

"We began in 1869 with a capacity of 1,000 barrels a day. At the start everything was *couleur de rose*, so much so that we put our works in splendid shape. We manufactured all the products. We even got it down to making wax, and using the very last residuum in the boilers. We got the works in magnificent order and used up everything. We began to feel the squeeze in 1872. We did not know what was the matter. Of course we were all affected the same way In Pennsylvania, and of course we commenced shifting about, and meeting together, and forming delegations, and going down to Philadelphia to see the Pennsylvania Railroad, meeting after meeting and delegation after delegation. We suspected there was something wrong, and told those men there was something wrong somewhere; that we felt, so far as position was concerned, we had the cheapest barrels, the cheapest labour, and the cheapest coal, and the route from, the crude district was altogether in our favour. We had a railroad and a river to bring us our raw material. We had made our Investment based on the seaboard routes, and we wanted the Pennsylvania Railroad to protect us. But none of our meetings or delegations ever amounted to anything. They were always repulsed In some way, put off, and we never got any satisfaction. The consequence was that in two or three years there was no margin or profit. In order to overcome that we commenced speculating, in the hope that there would be a change some time or other for the better. We did not like the Idea of giving up the ship. Now, during these times the Standard Oil Company increased so perceptibly and so strong that we at once recognised it as the element. Instead of looking to the railroad I always looked to the Standard Oil Company. In 1874, I went to see Rockefeller to find if we could make arrangements with him by which we could run a portion of our works. It was a very brief interview. He said there was no hope for us at all. He remarked this—I cannot give the exact quotation—'There is no hope for us,' and probably he said, 'There is no hope for any of us but he says, 'The weakest must go first.' And we went."

From The Jungle, *Upton Sinclair, 1906*

The Jungle is a novel by Pulitzer Prize–winning author Upton Sinclair (1878–1968) about the corruption of the American meatpacking industry during the early twentieth century. Sinclair harshly depicts the poverty, absence of social programs, unpleasant living and working conditions, and hopelessness prevalent among the poor working class.

The Jungle is also an important example of the **muckraking** tradition. Sinclair wanted to persuade his readers that the mainstream American political parties offered little means for **progressive** change. This excerpt describes the conditions in which hogs were slaughtered.

“Entering one of the Durham buildings, they found a number of other visitors waiting; and before long there came a guide, to escort them through the place. They make a great feature of showing strangers through the packing plants, for it is a good advertisement. But Ponas Jokubas [a laborer at the meatpacking plant] whispered maliciously that the visitors did not see any more than the packers wanted them to. They climbed a long series of stairways outside of the building, to the top of its five or six stories. Here was the chute, with its river of hogs, all patiently toiling upward; there was a place for them to rest to cool off, and then through another passageway they went into a room from which there is no returning for hogs.

It was a long, narrow room, with a gallery along it for visitors. At the head there was a great iron wheel, about twenty feet in circumference, with rings here and there along its edge. Upon both sides of this wheel there was a narrow space, into which came the hogs at the end of their journey; in the midst of them stood a great burly Negro, bare-armed and bare-chested. He was resting for the moment, for the wheel had stopped while men were cleaning up. In a minute or two, however, it began slowly to revolve, and then the men upon each side of it sprang to work. They had chains which they fastened about the leg of the nearest hog, and the other end of the chain they hooked into one of the rings upon the wheel. So, as the wheel turned, a hog was suddenly jerked off his feet and borne aloft.

At the same instant the car was assailed by a most terrifying shriek; the visitors started in alarm, the women turned pale and shrank back. The shriek was followed by another, louder and yet more agonizing—for once started upon that journey, the hog never came back; at the top of the wheel he was shunted off upon a trolley, and went sailing down the room. And meantime another was

(continues)

(continued)

swung up, and then another, and another, until there was a double line of them, each dangling by a foot and kicking in frenzy—and squealing. The uproar was appalling, perilous to the eardrums; one feared there was too much sound for the room to hold—that the walls must give way or the ceiling crack. There were high squeals and low squeals, grunts, and wails of agony; there would come a momentary lull, and then a fresh outburst, louder than ever, surging up to a deafening climax. It was too much for some of the visitors—the men would look at each other, laughing nervously, and the women would stand with hands clenched, and the blood rushing to their faces, and the tears starting in their eyes.

Meantime, heedless of all these things, the men upon the floor were going about their work. Neither squeals of hogs nor tears of visitors made any difference to them; one by one they hooked up the hogs, and one by one with a swift stroke they slit their throats. There was a long line of hogs, with squeals and lifeblood ebbing away together; until at last each started again, and vanished with a splash into a huge vat of boiling water. ”

American Antiquities Act, 1906

President Theodore Roosevelt (1901–1906) strongly supported the American Antiquities Act of 1906. This law gave the president the power to set aside land for national parks and identify other places and sites as national monuments. The law established the basis of America's modern National Park System.

“ Be it enacted by the Senate and House of Representatives of the United States of America in Congress assembled, That any person who shall appropriate, excavate, injure, or destroy any historic or prehistoric ruin or monument, or any object of antiquity, situated on lands owned or controlled by the Government of the United States, without the permission of the Secretary of the Department of the Government having jurisdiction over the lands on which said antiquities are situated, shall, upon conviction, be fined in a sum of not more than five hundred dollars or be imprisoned for a period of not more than ninety days, or shall suffer both fine and imprisonment, in the discretion of the court.

Sec. 2. That the President of the United States is hereby authorized, in his discretion, to declare by public proclamation historic landmarks, historic and prehistoric structures, and other objects of historic or scientific interest that are situated upon the lands owned or controlled by the Government of the United States to be national monuments, and may reserve as a part thereof parcels of land, the limits of which in all cases shall be confined to the smallest area compatible with proper care and management of the objects to be protected: Provided, That when such objects are situated upon a tract covered by a bona fied unperfected claim or held in private ownership, the tract, or so much thereof as may be necessary for the proper care and management of the object, may be relinquished to the Government, and the Secretary of the Interior is hereby authorized to accept the relinquishment of such tracts in behalf of the Government of the United States.

Sec. 3. That permits for the examination of ruins, the excavation of archaeological sites, and the gathering of objects of antiquity upon the lands under their respective jurisdictions may be granted by the Secretaries of the Interior, Agriculture, and War to institutions which the may deem properly qualified to conduct such examination, excavation, or gathering, subject to such rules and regulation as they may prescribe: Provided, That the examinations, excavations, and gatherings are undertaken for the benefit of reputable museums, universities, colleges, or other recognized scientific or educational institutions, with a view to increasing the knowledge of such objects, and that the gatherings shall be made for permanent preservation in public museums.

Sec. 4. That the Secretaries of the Departments aforesaid shall make and publish from time to time uniform rules and regulations for the purpose of carrying out the provisions of this Act.

Approved, June 8, 1906

Glossary of Key Terms

abolitionist One who campaigned to abolish, or do away with, slavery.

abstinence The act or practice of refraining from drinking alcoholic beverages.

amendment An official change to a document, such as the U.S. Constitution.

anarchist One who believes in or advocates the abolishment of government in all forms.

antitrust Opposition to business organizations such as trusts and monopolies.

capitalism; capitalist system An economic system in which wealth, and the means of producing wealth, such as industry, are owned by private individuals rather than by a governmental entity or the people collectively.

Central powers The nations of Germany, Austria-Hungary, Turkey, and Bulgaria who fought against the Allies—Great Britain, France, Italy, and others—during World War I (1914–1918).

child labor laws Acts of Congress that attempted to prevent or restrict the use of child workers in factories and other industries.

communism Form of government in which all means of production—land, labor, and capital—is owned by the people.

Communist; Communist Party A person or policy that advocates a form of government in which all means of production is owned by the people; a political party.

conservation The management of natural resources, such as land and water, to prevent waste and preserve them for future generations.

conservatives Individuals opposed to rapid change in society.

corporation A business owned by individuals who invest in that company.

corruption Obtaining advantage through illegal or immoral means.

democracy A form of government in which the citizens elect their leaders.

electoral votes Ballots cast by members of the Electoral College for the office of U.S. president.

electorate The voters.

emancipation Liberation; freedom from slavery.

eminent domain The right of the state to take private property for public use.

excise tax A tax on goods produced within a country.

exposé A type of reporting in which journalists reveal corruption or misconduct.

feminism The belief that women have the same political and social rights as men.

idealism The act or practice of picturing things in their ideal or perfect form.

immigrants People who move away from their country of origin and settle in a different country.

imperialist A person or policy that advocates the expansion of a nation's power through the acquisition of colonies.

incumbent The person who currently holds a political office.

Industrial Revolution The dramatic change from making goods by hand at home to making them by machine in factories.

initiative The procedure by which citizens can propose a law.

isolationist A person or policy that advocates minimal involvement in world affairs.

kangaroo court A court characterized by irresponsible, unauthorized, or irregular status or procedures.

laissez–faire A term that describes a government policy of little involvement in the economy.

lame duck A person holding political office after his or her replacement has been elected to the office but before the current term has ended.

legislature The branch of government that make laws.

lynching Putting a person to death by a mob without due process of law.

middle class The social class between the upper and lower classes, usually consisting of business or professional people.

monopoly A company that controls an entire industry.

muckrakers Progressive journalists who dug up the "muck," or dirt, of society, in the late 1800s and early 1900s.

natural law Eighteenth-century theory based on the belief that there is a natural or reasonable order to things.

naturalist A person who appreciates the beauty and natural wonder of nature and who favors conservation.

New Deal Name given to the policies advocated by President Franklin D. Roosevelt (1933–1945) that were aimed at ending the economic crisis known as the Great Depression.

organized crime The operation of illegal business entities whose members are bound together because of their group interest and their desire to profit from illegal activity.

partisanship An inclination to favor one group or view or opinion over alternatives.

patent A document granting an inventor sole rights to an invention.

platform A document stating the aims and principles of a political party.

political machine An organized group that controls the activities of a political party with the intention of maintaining that party in power.

Populist Party A political party formed in 1891 to represent the interests of farmers.

primary elections Elections in which voters choose from among a slate of candidates who will be the official party nominees in upcoming regular elections.

Progressives; Progressive Individuals who favor reform, or change; favoring reform.

prosecutor A government official who conducts criminal legal proceedings on behalf of the state.

Quakers People who belong to a Christian religious denomination known as the Religious Society of Friends.

ratification Official confirmation of a treaty or other such document by the U.S. Senate.

rebate A refund of some fraction of the amount paid.

recall The power of the voters, through the right of petition, to attempt to remove an elected government official.

referendum Submission of a proposed law to direct popular vote.

reform A movement aimed at removing political or social abuses.

regiment A troop of army soldiers.

regulation Rules and laws by which businesses must abide.

segregation The separation of groups, especially based on race.

socialism In Marxist theory, the type of governmment that appears after the proletariat, or workers, takes over the means of production, but before the state withers away and true communism is achieved; the state owns all property and controls the economy.

Socialist Party A political party in the United States that advocated public ownership of major industries, such as the railroads, the oil industry, and the steel industry.

social worker A person whose work applies social theory and research methods to study and improve the lives of people, groups, and society.

suffrage The right to vote.

sweatshop A small, crowded factory where people work in unsafe conditions.

tariff Tax on imported products.

taxidermy The process of preparing animal skins and stuffing them in lifelike forms.

tenements Buildings for human habitation that are, in general, run-down and whose facilities and maintenance barely meet minimum standards.

territory A geographical area under the jurisdiction of a sovereign state.

third-party candidate A person running for office who is not a member of either of the two major political parties—the Democratic Party and Republican Party.

timberland Land that is covered with trees and shrubs.

transcript A written record of dictated or recorded speech.

trust A group of independent organizations formed to limit competition by controlling the production and distribution of a product or service.

unethical Not conforming to approved standards of social or professional behavior.

unpatriotic Showing a lack of love or devotion to one's country.

veto The power of the president to reject a law passed by Congress.

workers' compensation Payments made to workers who have lost their jobs.

Selected Bibliography

Adams, Katherine H., and Michael L. Keene. *Alice Paul and the American Suffrage Campaign.* Champaign: University of Illinois Press, 2007.

Addams, Jane. *Twenty Years at Hull House.* New York: New American Library Classics, 1999.

Anderson, Judith Icke. *William Howard Taft: An Intimate History.* New York: W.W. Norton & Company, 1981.

Anthony, Susan B. *The Trial of Susan B. Anthony.* Amherst, N.Y.: Humanity Books, 2003.

Arthur, Anthony. *Radical Innocent: Upton Sinclair.* New York: Random House, 2006.

Auchincloss, Louis. *Theodore Roosevelt.* New York: Times Books, 2002.

Baker, Jean A. *Sisters: The Lives of American Suffragists.* New York: Hill & Wang, 2006.

Barry, Kathleen. *Susan B. Anthony: A Biography of a Singular Feminist.* Bloomington, Ind.: 1st Books Library, 2000.

Bausum, Ann. *Muckrakers: How Ida Tarbell, Upton Sinclair, and Lincoln Steffens Helped Expose Scandal, Inspire Reform, and Invent Investigative Journalism.* Des Moines, Iowa: National Geographic Children's Books, 2007.

Benson, Michael. *William Howard Taft.* Minneapolis, Minn.: Lerner Publications, 2007.

Berson, Robin. *Jane Addams: A Biography.* Westport, Conn.: Greenwood Press, 2004.

Bohannon, Lisa Frederkisen. *Failure Is Impossible: The Story of Susan B. Anthony.* Greenville, N.C.: Morgan Reynolds, 200l.

Brands, H.W. *Woodrow Wilson.* New York: Times Books, 2003.

Cefrey, Holly. *The Sherman Antitrust Act: Getting Big Business Under Control.* New York: Rosen Publishing, 2003.

Chace, James. 1912: *Wilson, Roosevelt, Taft and Debs—The Election That Changed the Country.* New York: Simon & Schuster, 2005.

Clift, Eleanor. *Founding Sisters and the Nineteenth Amendment.* New York: Wiley, 2003.

Cooper, John Milton, Jr. *Woodrow Wilson: A Biography.* New York: Knopf, 2009.

Crook, Paul. *Darwin's Coat-Tails: Essays on Social Darwinism.* New York: Peter Lang Publishing, 2007.

Dickens, Peter. *Social Darwinism: Linking Evolutionary Thought to Social Theory.* London: Open University Press, 2000.

Dudley, William. *Social Justice.* Farmington Hills, Mich.: Greenhaven Press, 2005.

Eisenach, Eldon J., ed. *The Social and Political Thought of American Progressivism.* Indianapolis, Ind.: Hackett Publishing, 2006.

Flanagan, Maureen A. *America Reformed: Progressives and Progressivisms, 1890s-1920s.* New York: Oxford Books, 2006.

Fradin, Dennis Brindall, and Judith Bloom Fradin. *Jane Addams: Champion of Democracy.* New York: Clarion Books, 2006.

Freedman, Russell. *Kids at Work: Lewis Hine and the Crusade Against Child Labor.* Boston: Clarion Books, 1994.

Garraty, John. *Teddy Roosevelt: American Rough Rider.* New York: Sterling, 2007.

Giddings, Paula J. *Ida: A Sword Among Lions: Ida B. Wells and the Campaign Against Lynching.* New York: Amistad Press, 2008.

Gifford, Catolyn De Swarte, and Amy R. Slagell, eds. *Let Something Good Be Said: Speeches and Writings of Frances E. Willard.* Champaign: University of Illinois Press, 2007.

Ginzberg, Lori. *Elizabeth Cady Stanton: An American Life.* New York: Hill and Wang, 2009.

Glowacki, Peggy, and Julia Hendry. *Hull House.* Mount Pleasant, S.C.: Arcadia Publishers, 2004.

Goldberg, Vicki. *Lewis W. Hine: Children at Work.* New York: Prestel Publishing, 1999.

Gore, Al. *An Inconvenient Truth: The Crisis of Global Warming*. New York: Viking Juvenile, 2007.

Gornick, Vivian. *The Solitude of Self: Thinking About Elizabeth Cady Stanton.* New York: Farrar, Strauss, & Giroux, 2006.

Gould, Lewis L., ed. *Bull Moose on the Stump: The 1912 Campaign Speeches of Theodore Roosevelt.* Lawrence: University of Kansas Press, 2008.

Gould, Lewis L. *The William Howard Taft Presidency.* Lawrence: University of Kansas Press, 2009.

Grace, Fran. *Carry A. Nation: Retelling the Life.* Bloomington: Indiana University Press, 2008.

Greenland, Paul R., and Annamarie L. Sheldon. *Career Opportunities in Conservation and the Environment.* New York: Checkmark Books, 2007.

Harmon, Daniel E. *Al Gore and Global Warming.* New York: Rosen Publishing, 2008.

Harmon, Daniel E., and Arthur M. Schlesinger. *The Food and Drug Administration. (How Your Government Works).* New York: Chelsea House, 2002.

Hindman, Hugh D. *Child Labor: An American History.* New York: M.E. Sharpe, 2002.

Jacob Riis Park. Available online: http://nyharborparks.org/visit/jari2.html

Jane Addams Hull House Association. Available online: http://www.hullhouse.org

John Muir Trail. Available online: http://johnmuirtrail.org

Kahn, Gordon, and Al Hirschfield. *The Speakeasies of 1932.* Milwaukee, Wis.: Glenn Young/Applause Books, 2005.

Kaplan, Justin. *Lincoln Steffens.* New York: Simon & Schuster, 2004.

Koutras Bozonelis, Helen. *A Look at the Nineteenth Amendment: Women Win the Right to Vote.* Berkeley Heights, NJ: Enslow Publishers, 2008.

Kraft, Betsy Harvey. *Theodore Roosevelt: Champion of the American Spirit.* New York: Clarion Books, 2003.

Learner, Michael A. *Dry Manhattan: Prohibition in New York City.* Cambridge, Mass.: Harvard University Press, 2008.

Lieurance, Suzanne. *The Prohibition Era in American History.* Berkeley Heights, N.J.: Enslow Publishers, 2003.

Linn, James Weber. *Jane Addams: A Biography*. Champaign: University of Illinois Press, 2000.

Loos, Pamela. *Elizabeth Cady Stanton.* New York: Chelsea House, 2001.

Lower, Richard. *A Bloc of One: The Political Career of Hiram W. Johnson*. Stanford, Calif.: Stanford University Press, 1993.

Lucas, Eileen. *The Eighteenth and Twenty-First Amendments: Alcohol—Prohibition and Repeal.* Berkeley Heights, N.J.: Enslow Publishers, 1998.

Lukes, Bonnie L. *Woodrow Wilson and the Progressive Era.* Greensboro, N.C.: Morgan Reynolds Publishing, 2005.

Maynard, W. Barksdale. *Woodrow Wilson*. New Haven, Conn.: Yale University Press, 2008.

McNeese, Tim. *The Progressive Movement: Advocating Social Change.* New York: Chelsea House, 2007.

——. *The Robber Barons and the Sherman Antitrust Act: Reshaping*

American Business. New York: Chelsea House, 2008.

Miller, Char. *Gifford Pinchot and the Making of Modern Environmentalism.* Washington, D.C.: Island Press, 2004.

Muir, John. *The Wilderness World of John Muir.* New York: Mariner Books, 2001.

Norris, George. *Fighting Liberal: The Autobiography of George W. Norris.* Lincoln: University of Nebraska Press, 1992.

Pappas, Christine. *Fighting Statesman: Senator George Norris.* Kansas City, Mo.: Acorn Books, 2001.

Patsouras, Louis. *Thorstein Veblen and the American Way of Life.* Tonawanda, N.Y.: Black Rose Press, 2004.

Pestritto, Ronald J. *American Progressivism: A Reader.* Lanham, Md.: Lexington Books, 2008.

Phillips, Kevin. *William McKinley.* New York: Times Books, 2003.

Roosevelt, Theodore. *Theodore Roosevelt: An Autobiography.* New York: Dodo Press, 2006.

Rossi, Anne. *Created Equal: Women Campaign for the Right to Vote 1840–1920.* Washington, D.C.: National Geographic Children's Books, 2005.

Sinclair, Upton. *The Jungle.* New York: Simon & Schuster, 2004.

Slavicek, Louise Chipley. *The Prohibition Era: Temperance in the United States.* New York: Chelsea House, 2008.

Stalcup, Brenda, ed. *Susan B. Anthony.* Farmington Hills, Mich.: Greenhaven Press, 2001.

Stanton, Elizabeth Cady. *The Woman's Bible: A Classic Feminist Perspective.* Mineola, N.Y.: Dover Publications, 2003.

Steen, Harold K. *The U.S. Forest Service: A History.* Seattle: University of Washington Press, 2004.

Steffens, Lincoln. *The Autobiography of Lincoln Steffens.* Berkeley, Ca.: Heyday Books, 2005.

——. *The Shame of the Cities.* Mineola, N.Y.: Dover, 2004.

Theodore Roosevelt Association. Available online: http://www.theodoreroosevelt.org/life/lifeoftr.htm

Todd, Anne M. *Susan B. Anthony.* New York: Chelsea House, 2009.

Unger, Nancy C. *Fighting Bob La Follette: The Righteous Reformer.* Chapel Hill, N.C.: University of North Carolina Press, 2000.

Ward, Geoffrey. *Not for Ourselves Alone: The Story of Elizabeth Cady Stanton and Susan B. Anthony.* New York: Knopf, 2001.

Weinberg, Steve. *Taking on the Trust: The Epic Battle of Ida Tarbell and John D. Rockefeller.* New York: W.W. Norton & Company, 2008.

William Howard Taft Museum. Available online: http://www.nps.gov/wiho/index.htm

Women's Rights National Park. Available online: http://www.nps.gov/wori/index.htm

Woodrow Wilson Presidential Library. Available online: http://www.woodrowwilson.org/visit/

Worster, Donald. *A Passion for Nature: John Muir.* New York: Oxford University Press, 2008.

Yochelson, Bonnie, and Daniel Czitrom. *Rediscovering Jacob Riis: The Reformer, His Journalism, and His Photographs.* New York: New Press, 2008.

Young, James Harvey. *Pure Food: Securing the Federal Food and Drug Act of 1906.* Princeton, N.J.: Princeton, University Press, 1998.

Index

Page numbers in **boldface** indicate topics covered in depth in the **A** to **Z** section of the book.